# CASSANDRA EASON
# PSYCHIC POWER OF CHILDREN
### and how to deal with it

# CASSANDRA EASON PSYCHIC POWER OF CHILDREN

## and how to deal with it

quantum

LONDON • NEW YORK • TORONTO • SYDNEY

# quantum

An imprint of W. Foulsham & Co. Ltd
The Publishing House, Bennetts Close, Cippenham, Slough,
Berkshire, SL1 5AP, England


ISBN 0-572-03061-4

Copyright © 2005 Cassandra Eason

Cover photograph by Jurgen Ziewe

A CIP record for this book is available from the British Library

The moral right of the author has been asserted

Printed in Great Britain by Creative Print and Design (Wales), Ebbw Vale

# Contents

# Children and Psychic Powers

It is 15 years since I wrote my first book on psychic children and ten years since my last rewrite. Since then I have received hundreds of letters, phone calls and e-mails from concerned parents and from adults who still recall their own psychic experiences from childhood as clearly as if they were yesterday. In those 15 years, too, I have written more than 50 books on all aspects of psychic experience. Most of these experiences cannot be explained away in terms of psychology and reason.

I intended my first book on the subject of childhood psychic abilities to be a psychological study of the world of children based on my knowledge as a teacher, some psychology training and my experience as a mother of five, whom I tried, not very successfully, to raise according to good psychological practice, ignoring my own instincts – instincts and intuitions were for chickens and monkeys I naively believed. However, in spite of my best endeavours, I was unable to write the kind of book I had planned. As I listened to rational, down-to-earth mothers telling their amazing stories of their offspring's off-the-clock abilities, I ended up with more questions than answers and cases that defied explanation within my safe but inadequate frameworks. Indeed, as time goes on, I find that psychology becomes less and less satisfactory as a means to explain away the magical and wondrous world of childhood. Only now I am glad.

## The story of Jack

What changed it all? My middle son, Jack, who at the time was not yet three, managed in a single morning with a few seemingly insignificant words to upset my ordered world view – and to launch me on a new career that has taken me from America to Scandinavia, researching all kinds of inexplicable phenomena in adults as well as children.

'Daddy's gone poly-boys on his motor bike, but he's all right,' commented Jack on my life-changing morning and carried on with his breakfast. 'Poly-boys' was the playful expression I used when I rolled Jack on the floor while dressing him.

As Jack was speaking, the back wheel of my husband John's motorcycle hit a patch of oil and his bike skidded on the elevated section of the M4 motorway in west London. As predicted by my cereal-smeared seer, John was unhurt apart from a few cuts and bruises and a now rather more battered Honda VF750 motor cycle.

Rational explanations were unsatisfactory because the time of Jack's remark and the accident coincided precisely.

## The hidden world of childhood

From that single incident, a door swung open into an entirely hidden world of childhood psychic experience as I tried to understand how Jack could so accurately foretell what he could not physically see. As I researched children and psychic abilities, so mothers, especially, hesitantly shared with me similar incidents with their children. Other people recalled how as children they were disbelieved or even punished for trying to share their inexplicable experiences with their parents. Fifteen years on, though the subject is one that elicits a huge post bag after an article in a magazine or a radio interview, many who write to me say, 'Please do not mention my name.'

In spite of the many fictional children's teatime TV series on magical children or witches, the subject is still taboo. In schools we talk even to quite young children about sex, alcohol and drugs, but if a child mentions that the family home has a ghost or that he talks to a dead grandmother, many teachers are uncertain how to respond. At worst, alarm bells ring and psychologists or social workers are sent in to uncover what is usually not a family trauma but a loving grandma who can't resist popping back from the heavenly fields to check on the family. Unfortunately, parents – especially lone ones from lower socio-economic backgrounds – tend to be regarded with more suspicion if the child reports psychic activities in the home (the wealthy may be regarded as eccentric or over-imaginative). I speak as someone who has been a lone parent with very little money and who was born in the back streets of the industrial Midlands.

My own website is committed to answering letters, especially from teenagers who are worried about a strange experience or are uncertain how to handle a surge of psychic energy. Psychic powers are strongest in the pre-school years but settle down once the child enters the education system and is focused on developing logical analytical skills. However, just before adolescence, as the teenager's identity becomes more fluid and hormones kick in, psychic experiences re-emerge and, if badly handled, can be disturbing. This is a time when a teenager may need support as they confront issues of evil in the real world and realise that parents cannot always protect them from harmful influences and nasty situations.

*Buffy the Vampire Slayer* and other cult teen magic series, as well as less scrupulous teen spell books, can give even a sensible adolescent wrong ideas about perfectly natural psychic powers and may focus their minds unnecessarily on paranormal evil – which in real life is very rare.

In this book, cases include those of very young children whose experience is reported and sometimes interpreted by the mother and those of teenagers up to the age of 18. In fact, what I would class as adolescent psychic phenomena may continue right into the twenties, especially in young women, and so the sections on teenage psychic powers are also applicable to them.

## Researching psychic experience

Because the majority of childhood psychic experiences are entirely spontaneous and channelled through the emotions generated by the family link of love, they are remarkably difficult to research. Forget the much vaunted repeatability and controlled reliability demanded under laboratory conditions to confirm validity. There was no way that my son Jack's predictions could be re-run so they could be timed and measured and everyone's pulse rate tested (having been up all night with the baby prior to the incident, mine was practically non-existent).

Most experiments with children fail to reflect their true psychic potential because the tests are necessarily quite dull and trivial to allow for them to be repeated and the results compared across a wider sample of children. The average child naturally loses concentration under test conditions, while psychically gifted children become frustrated because their powers cannot be generated on demand and certainly not shaped to fit the experimental situation. They may then be accused of cheating in their original, more spontaneous, demonstration of power. There may, in addition, be clashes over acceptable test conditions. However, I have reported some tests that have succeeded in avoiding these problems.

The clashes between gifted children and scientists or sceptics have been ongoing since 1848, when, on 31 March, extensive testing of a case of childhood psychism took place for probably the first time. Two sisters, Margarita (Maggie) and Catherine Fox, successfully communicated with an entity that had been responsible for noisy night-time disturbances. The girls challenged their invisible communicator to make the corresponding numbers of raps in response to finger-snapping, clapping and noiseless movements of their hands; it did this. The girls discovered over a period of time that the spirit was a former peddler, Charles B Rosna, who had been murdered on the site in 1843 by a previous tenant, John C Bell, and buried in the cellar.

Their amazing ability to communicate directly with spirits led to the birth of spiritualism and organised mediumship. However, the cost of constantly demonstrating their psychic powers under pressure eventually destroyed the girls. Both ended their adult careers in alcoholism and underwent periods of despair, Maggie denying her original powers.

However, such problems are not a consequence for all psychic children exposed to the glare of publicity. I report in Chapter 10 the happier story of a Japanese boy healer, Takaaki Moor, who has coped well with fame and as a young adult still does remarkable work.

The years 2003–4 saw a series of televised clashes between super-sceptic James Randi and Mai Takahashi, a 14-year-old Japanese girl whose telepathic powers have brought her fame in Japan. Her method involves a small piece of paper bearing a Japanese character. This is folded over twice and then fastened to her right palm using a wrapping of transparent tape. A cloth bag is then placed over her right arm and tied with a drawstring near her elbow. After two encounters, Randi claimed she was a fake, but the televised programme did indicate some remarkable results by Takahashi in spite of the stressful situation and obvious disbelief of the tester.

### Chinese and Mexican super-children

According to researchers such as Paul Dong and Thomas Raffill, thousands of super-children have been discovered in China since 1985. When blindfolded, the children can apparently 'see' with their ears, nose, mouth, tongue, armpits, hands or feet. In one test, a page was ripped from one of a pile of books chosen at random, screwed into a ball and placed, for example, in the armpit of the child. The blindfolded child could read every word.

More than 1,000 children in Mexico City were found to have the same ability. In both places the children also apparently displayed amazing psychokinetic powers – the ability to move objects with their thoughts. Most significantly, they seemed to be able to teach other children to do the same.

### How to understand psychic powers in childhood

I believe the best way of understanding, rather than testing or demonstrating, children's innate abilities under artificial conditions is to collect and categorise actual spontaneous experiences as I have tried to do over the years. Sometimes there is a third party present, but anecdotal evidence in which a parent or child alone reports a psychic occurrence is in fact rich human experience, rooted in real situations and a particular context.

Questionnaires can be of value. The late Sir Alister Hardy, at whose research centre in Oxford I was an Honorary Research Fellow into childhood psychic and religious experience for three years, derived a great deal of information by this method. But the core of his material came from letters written often many years after a psychic event by people usually just wanting to have their experience accepted as of value. I corresponded with a number of these people.

## About this book

My own collection of material is now quite extensive and drawn from many parts of the world. Because I have added a large number of new accounts to this book, it has been hard to decide which material from the earlier two editions I can bear to leave out.

From 2001–3, I worked as a columnist with the women's magazine *Best,* answering letters from readers on the subject of psychic children. I have subsequently set up a website via which I now answer queries. Many letters have come from mothers who were concerned about a psychic child or had unresolved questions from their own childhood. I also receive reports of childhood psychic experiences when I speak about the subject on radio and television shows. For this edition of the book I also appealed for stories in a number of general newspapers, ranging from the *Vancouver Sun* in Canada to Southampton's *Southern Echo* in England, and received a large number of replies. Some of the respondents had continued to experience psychic phenomena throughout their lives.

In this book I do offer some comments on the accounts, all of which are direct reproductions or summaries of the correspondent's actual words. I have also ended each chapter with an advice section on how to handle a child's psychic experiences in the area under discussion. In the main, however, the experiences I have chosen speak for themselves, and I am aware of how special they are and what a privilege it is to be allowed to share them with others.

Because many people still do not talk about their own or their children's psychic experiences, it is all too easy to feel isolated and worried that your child is different, as I did immediately after Jack's experience. Some older people especially may have painful memories of a badly handled psychic incident in childhood. By sharing it, they are able to have acknowledged what they know was true.

## Psychically gifted children

Since the previous edition of this book, some researchers have attempted to categorise children's spirituality and psychic potential to explain how current social trends for children may reflect deeper spiritual origins. I have described the Star child theory in Chapter 7. Here I will briefly describe Indigo and Crystal children. If you would like to find out more, there is much material on the internet – enter 'indigo children' or 'crystal children' on a good search engine. There are also books listed in Recommended Reading (see page 186).

### Indigo children

'Indigo' is a term applied to millions of children worldwide who are said to possess one of the higher spiritual colours, indigo, in their aura (the psychic energy field that surrounds them). This may be seen clairvoyantly around the head and shoulders.

These children have all been born since the mid-1970s. They are described as very wise, intelligent and sensitive, but they may not perform well in conventional schooling. It has been claimed that many Indigo children are misdiagnosed as having Attention Deficit Hyperactive Disorder, because they cannot accept society as it is and so rebel and behave anti-socially. Talking like adults from a very young age and questioning everything are other traits that can put them at odds with authority early on – but make them exciting to teach and parent. If well handled, Indigos become great channels for creative change, and their autocratic natures, expressed from infancy, can make them excellent leaders when they grow up.

Jan Carroll and Lee Tober first wrote about Indigo children in 1999, claiming they were born to bring in a new age of peace and tolerance. Whether or not you accept this view – and there are many complex social and educational reasons for the increase in hyperactivity and anti-social behaviour among children – crystals, a recommended therapy for Indigos, have been found to calm hyperactive children and improve their focus. My own Indigo baby, Bill, declared uneducable and totally disruptive at the age of five, is now at 16 taking his A Levels at college.

### Crystal children

Doreen Virtue, best known for her work with angels, has recently written about a new generation of children being born now whose auras are more opalescent and radiant than those of Indigo children. These Crystal children are psychic, wise and sensitive like the Indigo children and often report past lives or talk about distant galaxies. However, they are much gentler than Indigos and appear very still and serene. When working in various crystal stores, I have myself noticed that a number of quite tiny children in pushchairs will sit totally motionless, not attempting to touch anything, transfixed by a hanging crystal for quite long periods. While I work with their parents, they will sit quietly for half an hour or so, playing with my crystal spheres and small crystals with amazing gentleness.

In Chapter 1, I will describe children's telepathic experiences and attempt to explain this widespread but amazing ability.

# Twenty-five Ways to Know If Your Child Has Psychic Powers

Read through the following list and tick any that apply to your child.

1 Your child knows exactly what you are thinking, even though you are sure you did not speak aloud or you are in another part of the house.

2 Your child will tell you who is phoning before you pick up the receiver.

3 Your child will get upset or refuse to go into certain buildings where you later discover a tragedy had occurred years before.

4 Your child will describe an old man or woman who comes at night to tell them stories. You find out that the person lived in your house many years before and usually died peacefully there.

5 Your child talks about where and when they lived before they were born or will describe in detail a place they have never visited before.

6 Your child has or had an invisible friend who tells them something the child could not have possibly known about the place or time the friend comes from.

7 Your child talks about shining lights and colours round people's heads.

8 Your child insists they can fly in dreams or float down the stairs.

9 Your child will pick up a crystal or put a hand on your head and instantly relieve your headache.

10 A normally active toddler or baby will sit motionless, smiling and pointing at what seems to be an empty space.

11 Your child will talk to someone you cannot see, leaving gaps in the conversation for answers. When questioned about their visitor, they will accurately describe a deceased relative who died before they were born and whose picture they have never seen.

**12** Your child will tell you they dreamed about a friend or relative or saw them and news will come about the person before the morning is over.

**13** Your child hears whispering in the grass or speaks about little brown or green figures in the garden or even in the middle of a town square.

**14** Your child accepts angels as part of their everyday life.

**15** A child will suddenly warn you that a car is coming round the corner too fast and that you should slow down, so averting an accident.

**16** Your child knows what is round an unfamiliar corner when you are out walking or can describe the next place on an unfamiliar bus or railway journey.

**17** In old churches or ruined abbeys your child may talk about ladies and men in funny, long, black or brown clothes and ask if you can hear the singing.

**18** Your child will suddenly smell tobacco in an old house and ask you who the man was smoking the funny white pipe.

**19** Your child is always surrounded by animals and often finds sick ones to bring home.

**20** If you are lost in an unfamiliar town, your child will generally know the way.

**21** Things seem to move by themselves when your child is cross or very excited.

**22** If your child is in daycare or staying with a relative, they will come to the door about five minutes before you arrive, even if you have no regular collecting pattern for your child.

**23** A normally sociable child will hide or refuse to speak to an apparently friendly person who subsequently proves to be bad news in your life.

**24** Your child says they can dance in front of their body or sit at the top of a tree without climbing it – usually they also describe something not visible from the ground.

**25** Your child can overhear conversations in other rooms or well beyond even the most acute range of hearing.

### How did you score?

If you ticked five or more of these statements, your child is displaying psychic powers. Encourage them to talk about their experiences and spend lots of time with them in the open air away from excessive artificial stimulation, such as theme parks, to allow their innate gifts to develop.

If you ticked ten or more statements, you have a very gifted child who may in the future show healing abilities and remain psychic all their lives. Be aware of their fears and help them to enjoy physical and mental activities as a counterbalance to their psychic gifts.

If you ticked 15 or more statements, you have a very special child. If you listen to them and try to see life through their eyes, they can teach you a great deal. But because they are very sensitive, they may need help to cope with the rough and tumble of the everyday world.

If your child did not score at all or scored below five, they may be very logical and practical. However, you can stimulate their imagination by encouraging quiet times rather than filling every moment with activity and learning or allowing them free access to games consoles and DVDs.

Younger children tend to score higher than school-age children, but, as I have already mentioned, there is often a surge of psychic activity in adolescence.

# CHAPTER I

# The Telepathic Link of Love

Telepathy, the ability to read another person's thoughts, is the most common childhood psychic ability. Most families have at least one extraordinary incident they can recall. In the earlier years a child tends to read a parent's mind, especially that of the mother. This is not entirely surprising, because the child was contained within the mother for nine months and their psyches continue to be joined for two or three years after the birth. For this reason too, a mother will often respond to a young child's distress even when she is not physically with her infant. I have written a great deal about the mother–child bond in *The Mother Link* (see page 187). In this chapter I focus on children receiving information telepathically, rather than transmitting it to their mothers or fathers.

But the telepathic link is not purely physical and genetic, for adopted children and their adoptive parents have similar bonds. However, adopted children may also link into the experiences of a birth mother whom they have never met. I have written about this later in the chapter.

As a child grows older and comes into contact with influences and experiences outside the family, thought-reading occurs with friends or even strangers. But always the link of love, the family bond, remains the primary and strongest source of mind-to-mind communication.

In this chapter I will give examples of spontaneous telepathic abilities. I will also make suggestions about how you can help your child to direct their telepathic mind power creatively. Finally, I will describe methods to maintain close psychic connections with your children if you travel away a lot or cannot live full-time with them because of marital breakdown.

Most telepathic experiences with children are not life or death revelations but are nevertheless remarkable because no words have been spoken. I would advise you to note them in a family journal when they occur, as the details blur over a remarkably short time.

### Maternal bonds

Carla, who lives in Cheshire, England, has four children. She remembers pushing the baby in the buggy with Dylan, then about four, trotting along beside her. As they walked, she was thinking of getting home, putting on her old but very comfortable red cord trousers and cycling round to her mother's house without the children so that she could get a bit of peace and quiet.

> I was at the crossroads and had a clear picture of myself riding back that way to Mum's. At that point Dylan piped up: 'Mum, why are you going on your bike in your red trousers to see Gran and not taking me?'

Travel featured in several experiences that were related to me, as did a state of relaxed silence between the adult transmitter and the child receiver of the telepathy. Doris was sitting on a train in Manchester, England, with her four-year-old daughter, Susan, on their way to see Doris's mother.

> We were waiting for the train to leave the station. Susan was looking at a comic and I was daydreaming. We were silent. My thoughts went to a journey I had made years before, at the time I was living in a house at Bosham Bay in Sussex. I had been on a trip to London and my feet were tired.
>
> On arriving at Bosham station, I had taken off my shoes to walk home. Now, sitting on the train in Manchester, all those years later, I recalled the exact sensation of walking down the road to the sea without shoes. I could feel the road under my stocking feet. Susan looked up from her comic. 'Why do you never let me walk down the road without shoes?' she asked.

In both cases, the mother was picturing a scene in her mind. Young children work best in images. Indeed, one young child, Dominic, told his mother, 'I can see pictures in your mind.' In both cases the mother was relaxed and open, and this quiet, almost mesmerised, state is especially conducive to childhood telepathy.

### Stress telepathy

Strong emotion is also a trigger to telepathic insights. Donata lives in Mainville, Ohio. Her daughter, now six, was born when Donata was 38.

> The intense birthing and bonding Hope and I experienced contributed to her abilities to communicate with me and her father on deep, unconventional levels.
>
> As early as a year, Hope could point to an object, particularly the bathtub drain handle. Within minutes it would break. Today she can often tell who is calling before I answer the phone or whether her father is home long before we pull into the driveway.
>
> When she was almost two, I went out for the afternoon leaving her at home with her sister. While on the Interstate highway, I was forced off the road by a truck. Although I was not injured, the incident was upsetting because the trucker did not stop.

> When I arrived home, Hope and I went out into the back yard to play in the sandbox. I sat in a lawn chair, vividly recalling the truck incident in my mind as I wrote a letter of complaint to the company whose truck had caused the near-accident. After a few minutes, my little girl who could barely talk, said, 'No big truck come in this yard, Momma.'
>
> I had not mentioned a word to Hope or her sister about the event concerning the truck, but Hope was able to pick up the information simply by being close to me. For days she assured me that our house and yard were safe from big trucks.

We do not know how early in life the child begins to home in on their mother's distress, but it is only when the child can put thoughts into words that we become aware of this. However, I believe that supporting mothers with babies or small children in practical ways would lessen their often unvoiced stress and result in calmer babies, thus lessening the need for more heavy-handed professional intervention later in the baby's life.

Mary, now a mother herself, living in County Cork, Ireland, can still recall this link between herself and her mother.

> When I was young, my mother had taken my brother to our summer place to do some work on the house. At about five o'clock in the afternoon, I knew something dreadful had happened to my mother. The feeling was so strong that I knelt down and started to pray. My mother sometimes had a tendency to choke, so my immediate thought was that it was that. But later I heard that she and my brother had gone for a walk to the beach and at about five o'clock she had fallen down the concrete steps leading on to the beach and hurt herself badly, though not dreadfully.

Mary also experienced the two-way radar linking mother to child. As in numerous cases I have researched, she was able to avert an accident by picking up her young child's intentions even though he was out of physical sight.

> I never had the feeling again till when my own son was about three. We had moved house and although we always meant to fit locks to the upstairs windows, we never got round to it. My mother and sister had come over and we were sitting having afternoon tea and chatting when I stopped mid-sentence. 'I've got to go to the little one,' I said and rushed upstairs to my husband's office, where my son was at the open window. He had climbed on to my husband's desk, somehow opened the window and was within two inches [5 centimetres] of falling out from the upper floor.

### Coming home

There has been excellent research into the ability of pets to anticipate their owner's arrival home by the Cambridge biologist Doctor Rupert Sheldrake, but there is none, as far as I know, into the ability of children to detect a mother or father's return.

Some mothers worry about their child's telepathic powers, often because, like maternal intuition, it is a subject largely ignored by conventional childcare experts and psychologists. Eminent professors can be equally foxed by the concept of mother–child psychic links. Indeed Robert M Sapolsky, Professor of Biological Sciences and Neuroscience at Stamford University, California, and author of the brilliant book *Why Zebras Don't Get Ulcers* (WH Freeman and Company, 1994) was less than forthcoming about maternal intuition when I asked him about it while researching an earlier book of my own: 'I don't have much to say about the issue of maternal love and intuition. As a scientist I am utterly puzzled by documented cases of that sort of thing.'

Kristin, who lives in North Vancouver, wrote:

When my daughter, now 16, was two, I was worried that she was psychic. I have since come to theorise that we are all born with an ability to communicate telepathically, but we lose it as we develop our language skills. As we become more dependent on the spoken word to communicate, our brains become 'hardwired', so to speak, and any psychic ability we may have had is lost for most of us.

When my daughter was two, she always announced the arrival home of her dad after work about two minutes before he set foot on the front steps. More alarming to me was the occasion when she was playing on the living room floor and I was reading the paper in the kitchen. She suddenly said out loud, word for word, the paragraph that I was reading. As her language skills increased, there was a corresponding decline in these apparently psychic events, and I was relieved.

Brenda, who also lives in Vancouver, was an independent witness to the bond between mother and child.

When my ninth grandchild was between the ages of one and two, she was often left with me for varying lengths of time while her busy mom did her chores. I would always spend the time playing with her or reading to her, and it was a time of togetherness and joy for both of us. But suddenly she would stop the activity in which we were engaged, look up, wait a couple of seconds, staring, and say 'Mamma?' And sure enough, in about three minutes her mom would drive into the driveway. I live on a very busy intersection, one road of which is the Trans Canada Highway. There is no way she could have identified her mother's car two or three blocks away. But she always knew when it was time to put away the toys or the book, ready for Mom's arrival.

In Ontario, Rebecca tries to make quiet moments during her working day in which she sends mental messages to her son in his crèche.

> Since my son, Alex, was born, we've had an amazing connection. He sleeps with my husband and me, but invariably since birth I've always awakened just before he does. Now that I'm back to work, Alex is in a daycare at my work site. Whenever I have a moment, I like to stop in my day and send him a mental 'I love you' message.
>
> The staff have commented that almost any time I call down by phone, Alex points and moves towards it when it's me, and only when it's me. When they buzz to let me in through the security door, Alex walks over to the gate as if he knows it's me. It doesn't matter what time of day I visit; he seems to know intuitively.
>
> I had often thought I'd work at my psychic connection with my children, but I am so busy that I never seemed to find the time, so I'm pleasantly surprised that my telepathic connection with Alex has developed effortlessly.

## Working with words

Gradually the child seems able to pick up thoughts in the form of words, and this forms the transition to telepathy with other adults and children, though pictures seem also to remain important to younger children.

Jo, from Nottingham, England, regularly experienced her daughter Hannah's mind-hopping. This is an account she sent me some years ago. Hannah's psychic powers became less noticeable once she was about seven, as do most children's. However, this is one of the best examples of continuing telepathy I have received.

> My daughter Hannah seems to read my thoughts, but it is always at a time of complete subconsciousness, i.e. we can't make it happen.
>
> One instance was when my husband was fixing the car. I was sitting on the bonnet of the car and Hannah was inside the car. I was thinking about age and about my parents getting older. Hannah wound the window down and said, 'Granddad's not old.'
>
> I asked her why she said that and she told me she just saw it.
>
> Hannah was about three years old at the time. There were lots of times when I was in one room wondering to myself whether Hannah would like something to eat and she would shout, 'Yes, please,' or 'No, thank you, Mummy.'
>
> One morning I was lying in bed. Hannah had got into bed next to me, and Andrew, my husband, was getting dressed. Andrew made us laugh, and I thought, 'Silly twit!'
>
> Hannah told me, 'Don't be rude, Mummy.'
>
> 'What do you mean?' I asked.
>
> 'Andrew's not silly,' she replied
>
> I often find that when I am reading something not out loud, just in my head, such as an article in a magazine, and Hannah is

around, she will add a comment that coincides with the topic. I tend to take it for granted now. As she is only just learning to read, it has to be a psychic thing.

Wendy from Hampshire, England, relates a similar ability:

I was washing my hair and thinking I hadn't seen my old bridesmaid, Julie, for some time. Within seconds my four-year-old daughter Jo piped up, 'When are we going to see Aunty Julie again, Mummy?' The friend had not been mentioned in conversation for some months and there was no reason why Jo should ask the question unless she was picking something up from me telepathically.

Jo also linked in with her father and was able to accurately predict his homecoming. My husband was serving a six-month tour with the RAF in Belize. We expected him home in June, but in April of that year Jo, who was four-and-a-half, insisted that her daddy would be coming home in May, and furthermore she said it would be on the 23rd. She was right.

## Loving Dad

In Jo's case the physical absence made no difference to the bond with her father. Hope, whom I mentioned a little earlier, was also very close to her father, who got involved when possible in her daily care. Hope and her father managed to communicate across the Atlantic. Hope was at home in Ohio with her mother Donata while her father was in England on a business trip. Donata says:

One morning at exactly 2.05 am (I checked the clock as I got up) Hope called me from her room. She sat bolt upright in bed, with eyes shining like headlamps. 'I hear something, Momma,' she said.

Hope rarely wakes up at night. If she does, she's groggy and simply rolls over and goes back to sleep. On this particular night, however, she was quite alert and repeated several times that she really could hear something. I reassured her and we both drifted off.

The next day, when her father called from London, he told me he had jogged that morning under a brilliant full moon. As he exercised, he asked the moon to shine her protective light down on his sleeping daughter. I confirmed the time with him. His lunar message was transmitted at exactly 7.05 am London time. With the five-hour time difference, her father's transatlantic tidings came to Hope the precise moment she woke.

However, even when the father has not been involved in daily care, strong emotion can, it seems, link the child and the absent parent. When the late Sir Peter Scott, naturalist, painter and sailor, was a young child, he is said to have told his mother: 'Daddy's stopped working.' He made this remark about the time his father, Captain Scott, died in the Antarctic in his bid to reach the South Pole. I asked Sir Peter about the story shortly before his death in 1989, and he wrote back:

> The story you describe was related to me in later years by my mother, who was very loath to believe that it had any significance, as she was always very sceptical of psychic phenomena. But the fact that she told me the story indicates, I think, that she was unwilling to dismiss the incident.

Did the boy in fact share his father's last moments? Sir Peter's mother, Kathleen Bruce, the sculptress who was to create the famous Peter Pan statue that stands in Kensington Gardens in London (J M Barrie, author of *Peter Pan*, was Sir Peter Scott's godfather), had no inkling of her husband's death, and it was six months before the frozen bodies of Scott and his companions were discovered.

But there is evidence that as death approached Captain Scott was thinking about his son. Among the letters he wrote during the time he was awaiting death in the snowbound tent, was one to J M Barrie, saying: 'I want you to help my widow and my son, your godson. Give the boy a chance in life if the state won't do it, he ought to have good stuff in him.' In his last diary, Scott writes that he hopes the boy will be made interested in natural history rather than games. In fact, Sir Peter proved equally skilled at both.

War also has triggered a number of the telepathic links I have documented over the years. During the retreat to Dunkirk, in the Second World War, Michael, a young army officer, was killed. Back home, in the countryside near Ipswich, his daughter, Fiona, was living with her grandmother, aunts and mother. She told them: 'Daddy came to me last night and told me to take care of Mummy.' The next day a telegram brought the news that her father had been killed.

Nor does the link have to be genetic. A stepfather or surrogate father can also be linked with a child's psychic thoughts, as can adoptive parents. Jan, from Wiltshire, England, explained:

> A year ago my fiancé, Paul, electrocuted himself and was taken to hospital. Fortunately, my two daughters were staying overnight with a friend and knew nothing of the accident.
>
> When they got home, Paul was there, although pretty shaken. As she came through the door, my seven-year-old, Elise, said, 'I had a funny dream about Paul last night. He was in a room with wires on his chest. The strange thing was he had pyjamas that colour,' and she pointed to a turquoise cushion. Paul had been given turquoise hospital pyjamas, as there had been no time to get anything of his own.

THE TELEPATHIC LINK OF LOVE

It's not the first such experience my daughter has had. Elise was not born while my mother was alive and yet she has seen her. She calls her 'my lady in the sky' and has described her in detail. Elise says the lady comes at Christmas and on birthdays to give her a kiss.

## Sibling links

Brothers and sisters also are joined telepathically. Though they may fight and argue, one will always respond to the other's distress even thousands of miles away. Dave wrote from Vancouver:

> When my son was eight and daughter 11, I travelled with my son alone to the UK from Vancouver to meet with my family. During the visit, he suddenly stopped in mid-stride and put his hand to his left shin and said, 'Joy's hurt!' Joy is his sister. I asked him what he meant, and he was very confused. I noted the time, and days later phoned my wife back in Vancouver, who related that at precisely that time Joy had fallen up the concrete steps and skinned her left leg very painfully.

The sibling psychic link can pick up good news too. Michael, who lives in Bethesda, Wales, told me:

> When my wife Sonia was in labour with our second child, we went to the hospital at nine in the morning, leaving our three-year-old son, Sammy, with a babysitter. At one minute past ten at night, Sammy told the babysitter that his baby brother had been born. That was the exact time the baby was born at the hospital, but we had not rung through with the news.

## Double trouble

The bond between twins is indisputable and is one of the few psychic links to have attracted research. Sharing pain is a very common phenomenon. In this first case, there were independent witnesses. James E Peron, Director of the US Childbirth Education Foundation, told me:

> I grew up with identical twin cousins eight months older than myself. I witnessed psychic communication between these brothers as a regular occurrence. Perhaps the most startling experience was when we were about 11 years old. We had been playing with neighbouring children in their farm barn, climbing to the upper beams of the barn and jumping into the hayloft. My cousin Dick and I returned home for our evening meal, but Donny remained playing with the neighbours' boys.
>
> We were sitting down at the dinner table when Dick suddenly bolted in his chair, screamed in pain and yelled, 'Donny's hurt. He fell backwards from the high beam in the barn and hurt his leg.'

> We rushed to the neighbouring farm. Donny had fallen at the precise moment that Dick had screamed, and had broken his leg rather severely. This was but one of many such experiences I witnessed with the boys. It was comical when we played Hide and Seek – they always knew where the other was hiding.

Peter, who lives in Kirkcudbright, Scotland, has identical twin daughters. He told me:

> Long before the twins could talk they were able to communicate with each other. It was amazing to watch them as they played. Sitting on the floor surrounded by toys, the girls would be chattering away to each other without any apparent meaning, not in an uncontrolled manner but very definitely in tune with each other. Louise would shriek and squeal at Victoria, who in return would pass something to her, and vice versa.
>
> There was a time when Louise developed an abscess under a tooth. Victoria also complained bitterly about a pain in her mouth. It stopped as soon as Louise's abscess was treated, but became really distressing while Louise was being treated some distance away.

Though the psychic bond between identical twins is understandable in genetic terms, non-identical twins can also be remarkably telepathic. Saga and Tuva are non-identical, three-year-old twin girls who live in central Sweden. Their mother, Susanne, a publisher, told me:

> Saga got her teeth earlier than Tuva by several months. But whenever Saga had a teething pain and a little red mark in her mouth where the tooth was coming and a fever, Tuva got precisely the same. It was just that no teeth came for poor Tuva. So I had double teething troubles. But when Saga's tooth was through, the red mark disappeared and Tuva was fine again till next time Saga was teething.
>
> When Saga goes down to the book packing warehouse at the bottom of our land with my husband Stefan, even though Tuva is quite happy playing with me, she will suddenly start crying. I know a second later the phone will ring and Stefan tell me Saga has fallen over or just started crying to come back up to the house because she is missing her sister.

### The link of loss

A young child can sense a sibling's death however much the adults involved try to hide the truth. Brenda, who lives in Andover, England, told me that she was about three when her younger brother George died.

> We lived in a very poor district and tuberculosis was rampant. My little brother George was in a sanatorium. One morning my grandma was looking after me while my parents were visiting when I

suddenly stopped playing and told her, 'George is in King Jesus' garden now.'

'No,' said my grandma, 'He's in hospital, but he's going to get better one day.'

But I still insisted, 'No, he's with King Jesus, picking flowers in his garden.'

When my mum and dad came home, they told my gran that my brother had died while they were with him at the time I had said. Grandma confirmed the story years later, but I can still remember Gran desperately trying to keep me round the back of the house on the day of the funeral and how I insisted on pushing my dolls' pram round to the street at the moment the hearse pulled up. Dad took me to look in a toyshop window while Mum and Gran were in church.

Fortunately, these days children are usually more closely involved in their siblings' illnesses, but it is rarely possible to hide the truth from a child.

## Bonds with Grandma

Though the strongest psychic bond is usually with the mother, there is also often a link with grandmothers. Corrine, who lives in Dorset, England, explained:

My daughter is five years old. My mum was at the birth of my daughter and, as I was ill, took care of her in the first few days, so there is a strong bond. My mum is in and out of hospital. Last October she went in for her 39th major operation.

One night my daughter Kayleigh woke up and said, 'Nanny isn't well.'

I replied, 'I know. She's in hospital.'

But she insisted, 'Nanny not well.'

Eventually I got her to go back to sleep. At midnight I received a phone call saying they couldn't contact my dad. My mother had been taken ill and was being rushed back into theatre. This, I feel, is what Kayleigh was trying to tell me.

Recently my mum was ill again. When she phoned up, Kayleigh answered the phone and said: 'You're better today, Nanny, aren't you?'

My mum replied that she was and asked how she knew. Kayleigh replied that she just knew when she woke up.

Kayleigh also had an imaginary friend who disappeared from her life when my grandma died before Christmas. Now she says she speaks to Great-nanny. My mum and I feel that it is nice and a comfort that she is watching over her.

I was told I couldn't have children. My sister died, and five weeks after her death I discovered I was five weeks pregnant. Kayleigh is a very special little girl to me.

Kayleigh's telepathic bond with her grandma, like my son Jack's with his father, seems rooted in the early hands-on care of the infant. But, of course, that is just one cause of such psychic closeness.

Anne, who lives in Christchurch, New Zealand, has close intuitive bonds into the fourth generation.

> I am a great-grandmother and very fond of my granddaughter. When her first baby was nearly due, she and her husband were dining with me one evening and suddenly I felt an overwhelming love and warmth for that little life sitting beside me and soon to be with us. I just knew that it was a little girl reaching out to me. All I could say was, 'Oh, I am looking forward to this baby.'
>
> That feeling has never left me, and a strong bond exists between me and the little girl, Melanie, who is five now and in her first year at school. She brings her drawings and first books to show me regularly and enjoys cuddles with her 81-year-old Little Grandma, as she calls me. When little Melanie was about four, she rang me up on a toy telephone from her home to say, 'Little Grandma, your lamp is falling down.'
>
> My granddaughter told me about this 'pretend conversation' later. However, Melanie had been right. At about that time my reading lamp had indeed overstrained its screws and fallen over my shoulders.

## Beyond the family

When children become older, they seem to turn their telepathic powers outwards towards the people they meet. Shaun, who comes from Dorset, England, described how:

> Just recently, whilst standing in a queue for a theme park ride, a couple of young girls made conversation with my six-year-old daughter Jessica. After a while, my daughter asked me to ask one of the girls what her name was. As I had heard her friend say it was Laura, I laughed and said I knew it was Laura.
>
> My daughter said that the girl didn't look like a Laura, but looked more like a Katie. The girl looked shocked and replied that her older sister was called Katie and that they were almost identical. When asked my daughter why she thought that, she just said that she knew.
>
> Jessica has also made comments with regard to a local church hall (these were when she was around two or three years old), saying that that was the place she used to dance in. We have never been in the place.

Jessica has perhaps been psychic for some time and was linking into a past life experience. Often details of this are tantalisingly few, but occasionally the evidence is very strong. I have written about past lives in Chapter 8.

At the age of six or seven, as the child becomes fully immersed in the world of school and physical activities, psychic activity generally recedes, to emerge again in adolescence as their certainties and their sense of self-identity come under question and hormones begin to rage.

Gillian, from London, England, wrote to me:

> When I was at junior school, I was walking home one summer afternoon and a boy unknown to me was walking in front. A voice inside my head kept saying, '"Martin", shout out, "Martin".' Thinking that if I did, I might look a fool, I just kept quiet. But this voice did not die down, so I decided to call out, believing that if no one turned round I would not lose face as there were plenty of people (adults as well as children) around.
>
> When I had called out, the boy turned round and asked me, 'How do you know my name?'

## How it works

There is no doubt that childhood telepathy does exist and is manifest regularly. However, scientific testing is difficult, because most examples of telepathy occur spontaneously, when the child is happy and relaxed or at a time of family crisis. However, there have been some successful tests.

Elaine Shrager PhD, of New York University, carried out tests in the 1980s. She hypothesised that young children would score highest on an ESP test if their own mother rather than another mother tried to send them a message. She carried out her experiments with 38 children aged three-and-a-half to five-and-a-half, using brightly coloured sweets. One hundred sweets, 20 each of five different colours, were placed in a brown paper bag. A mother shook the bag before each trial, selected one sweet without looking and then tried to transmit the colour mentally to a child, who was in another room. It was discovered that children whose own mother sent the telepathic message scored best

Equally impressive were the tests done by Professor Ernesto Spinelli, the Academic Dean of the School of Psychotherapy and Counselling at Regent's College, London, 15 years earlier. Professor Spinelli discovered that the younger the subject, the better they scored on telepathic tests. In two experiments, a large number of subjects aged between three and 70 years of age were divided into ten chronological age groups. Results showed highly significant scores among groups composed of subjects aged between three and eight years, but only chance level scores among groups in subsequent age groups. Results also indicated that within the three age groups that scored at above-chance levels, the youngest age group scored at significantly higher levels than the two other age groups and that the second youngest age group scored at levels significantly greater than the third age group. No significant differences between male and female scores in any of the ten age groups were observed.

Both these studies support the anecdotal evidence of childhood telepathy in everyday life. Dr Spinelli thinks that telepathic powers come from the same source as ordinary thought but that in the young child, this ability has not been suppressed by learning. Telepathic power, he believes, is a sort of externalised thinking that disappears once the child learns to do his thinking inside his head.

Dr Spinelli found that results were better when the children 'guessing' together were the same age, and even better when their IQs were the same. His results were just as good whatever kind of test the children were given. Commenting on the relaxation factor involved in real life telepathy, he told me when I interviewed him some years ago:

> My own feelings are that this is linked with the limitations of self-consciousness that are typically imposed but which become more blurred when one is in a relaxed, meditative or altered state.
>
> Since young children are only just beginning to have a clearly defined and restrictive sense of self, it is possible that their superior ability at telepathic tasks is a reflection of their open self-consciousness. Telepathy only strikes us as odd or unusual because we have a sense of self-consciousness – a notion that our thoughts are ours and ours alone.

## Teenagers and telepathy

Telepathy is less frequently reported by adolescents, who may work hard to keep their thoughts secret from parents and family. That teenagers do have strong psychic powers is shown throughout this book. Indeed, adolescent years are often a time of quite turbulent psychic phenomena in terms of premonitions, seeing ghosts or negative entities and poltergeist activity.

The majority of adolescent telepathic cases from my own research have been of mothers who have picked up telepathically on a teenager's danger, usually when they were somewhere they should not have been. I have come across far fewer examples of the opposite situation. It may be that teenagers are just more reluctant to report such incidents.

Hugh was 13 and at school in Liphook, England, when, at the end of the summer term, his father cycled up from their home in Southampton, 30 miles away, to see him. Hugh says:

> My father told me, 'I've found you a bicycle cape just like the one you wanted. I was cycling along and found it in front of me in the road. So I got off and picked it up.'
>
> I replied, 'Let me tell you where you found it. You were cycling up Weston Road away from our house towards The Avenue and it

was opposite the waste ground where the house has been pulled down and you found it about a yard from the kerb.'

'How did you know?' my father asked.

I had visualised the incident as he was telling me, but at the same time I felt sure that I was picturing what had actually happened.

This is an example of the kind of mind-to-mind transference that toddlers often experience. Hugh and his father were very close emotionally.

## When we were parted

One exception to the lack of reported teenage telepathy incidents is where a child is adopted. In this case, the teenage years may reawaken especially strong links between the adolescent and the mother they have not seen since birth, even if the teenager is not consciously searching for the birth mother.

Dr Lavonne Stiffler, the author of *Synchronicity and Reunion* (FEA Publishing, Florida, 1992) has carried out extensive research on the intuitive links between adopted children and natural parents from whom they were separated at birth. According to Dr Stiffler, the 'memory of a name the child never knew is particularly significant'. One adult adoptee told Dr Stiffler:

When I was a little girl and all through my teenage years I always wanted to be called Maggie. Not for any particular reason. I just always wanted that name. When I located my original name in the state's birth register, I found that it was Margaret. So I really was a Maggie all along.

Dr Stiffler sees this link as beyond our current understanding of genetics. 'The memory of a lullaby may have originated pre-natally. But from where originate the vivid dreams, the naming of an imaginary playmate or the strange drawing towards a particular location?'

Another adoptee told Dr Stiffler:

I always felt a piece of the puzzle was missing. It took me a long time to begin my search and it wasn't until it was over that I understood I had been guided all along. Throughout my life I was always triggered by an interest in sign language and I learned it from friends and people in my church. When I finally located her, Mom and I exchanged letters and pictures. Then she came to visit me and we met at the airport. I raised my hands in front of me in a gesture God had been preparing me for without my knowing why. Mom was deaf. We came closer. Carefully my hands signed the one beautiful word I'd longed to speak, 'Mother'.

Just as separated twins have unexplained links in their lives, so, according to Dr Stiffler, do birth mothers and children who have been apart. One mother told him:

> My daughter and I were both in bike accidents in 1971. She fell off her bike and broke her front tooth and I went flying over my bike and broke my front tooth. When she told me she had a cap on her front tooth, I said, 'So do I.'

### How to encourage telepathy

Try to spend quiet time together with your child, walking in the woods or local park or by the sea. Or carry out a routine task together, such as baking or gardening. This will give your psyches the space to connect. If you are tired and don't have the energy to tell a story before bed, make this a time when you listen to a gentle story tape or music or watch a familiar video, cuddled together.

During quiet times, think strongly of a pleasant scene in your past. Fill in the details in your mind, complete with colours and fragrances, and – since telepathy operates through emotional channels – recall the happy feelings. Ask the child if they can guess what pictures are in your mind. Keep notes of their descriptions.

If you are leaving a young child in a crèche, nursery school or daycare, take five minutes to look at a picture book with them in the morning and choose a picture you can both think of whenever you miss each other. Pick a simple, brightly coloured, linear image – a big red butterfly or a large blue house with yellow doors. Add a verbal message, such as 'Soon be home together' or 'Have fun', that the child will associate with the picture. If you can, also send the book along as a reminder. You can also swap twin tiny teddy bears, giving one to the child to take with them. Whenever they are sad or lonely, they can touch the bear and it will send a message to your bear to send some extra Mum or Dad love over the airwaves. This can be helpful if your child is staying away overnight, perhaps with a separated parent, and you are apprehensive.

If you are going to be late, as well as sending a verbal message for the child's carer to transmit, picture yourself hugging your child and share a telepathic cuddle. As you do so, tell the absent child in your mind when you will be back, for example after a favourite television programme has finished. Even a child who cannot tell the time will come to the door two or three minutes before you return.

If you cannot be with your child or phone them for several days because you live or work away or access is difficult after a divorce, arrange a time each day when you both send pictures in your mind of what you have been doing. Most of all, send love.

If you are separated from your child, keep a diary of every time you get a special feeling about them, including the date and time. Some day you may be able to match these moments up when you can be together with your child more frequently.

## When a child has a telepathic experience

Be glad that your child feels sufficiently close to you to tap into your thoughts, and take what your child reveals seriously. If your child has picked up on an absent relative's worries or sickness, check just in case.

Don't worry that your child is in some way odd, but help them to avoid embarrassing situations. Explain to your child that there are lots of ways of communicating, and reading thoughts is one that children are good at. Reassure them that the power can be very useful because you can know if a family member or friend far away is sad or not well. Tell them that if they pick up worrying thoughts they should tell you, and you will phone the person they are worried about and check that they are okay. At the same time, point out gently that grown-ups often like to keep their thoughts private, so the child should never shout out in public what someone is thinking or try to listen in deliberately, any more than they should listen in to an actual conversation.

With teenagers, tell them if you feel worried about them and create quiet times when they can share their psychic insights about your mutual lives. Adolescents are remarkably wise and can pick up all kinds of signals and undercurrents. In return you can offer them quiet advice based on psychic instincts.

# CHAPTER 2

# Children and Ghosts

After telepathy, ghost sightings are the most common childhood psychic experience. These can be more frightening for the parents than the child; however, this is an area where a sensitive parent can acknowledge the experience as valid and worthwhile, even if they themselves see nothing. Young children especially are naturally aware of other dimensions and may not differentiate between a living and a ghostly visitor. It is only as they reach school age and come into contact with the conventional view of ghosts as frightening that they become more apprehensive. In the 15 years since I wrote the first edition of this book, exposure to more sensational ghosts films on television has resulted in children reporting more negative ghost experiences.

Children most often see ghosts as solid and three-dimensional, perhaps because their physical and clairvoyant (or psychic) vision are not yet separate. Children also tend to think in images at least as much as words. The latter generally come to predominate as learning leads the child to structure thoughts and think more like an adult.

Ghost sightings can be divided into two main kinds: impressions of presences attached to specific places, and what seem to be actual ghosts, who may be family members or someone not known to the child.

## Ghostly images

Some presences are attached to a particular place, like a film recorded on a DVD, or an elaborate light show in which three-dimensional images are built up by the convergence of beams from different projectors. These apparitions are activated at certain times associated with dramatic events in the earthly life of the ghost, such as the anniversary of a fatal accident. Natural subterranean earth energy lines, called ley lines, also seem to give phantoms the power to manifest. Children, being very sensitive, are far more likely to perceive a ghostly image, and often a number of children and sensitive adults will describe the same ghost over a period of time

Since writing the previous two editions of this book, I have extensively researched auras, or psychic energy fields, and discovered that where there has been intense emotion generated in a house or on the land on which it is built, then impressions of the people and the events that triggered those emotions become imprinted on the walls or filter upwards through the land. Sometimes, too, a person's energies can become imprinted in emotionally significant artefacts that they owned. Holding the object can release awareness of, or an image of, the former owner. Adults as well as children experience these phenomena but may doubt the validity of the information they are receiving and so block it psychologically.

## Ghosts who return

By far the most common ghosts seen by children are personalised ones, who reflect the essential personality of the deceased person and interact with the child who sees them. These are often deceased grandmothers or grandfathers who return to visit or watch over a child and often become a kind of spirit guide. I have written more about invisible friends in Chapter 4 and spirit guides in Chapter 5. Children may also see former residents of their home, usually an old person who died there, and can usually describe the figure even though they have never seen the person, who may have died many years before.

Though many childhood ghosts are verifiable either by an independent witness or by subsequent research, some are never identified. This does not mean they are not real, and – as I explain on page 50 – to doubt or reject what a child reports is very hurtful for the child who is convinced of what they have seen and may need reassurance that ghosts are not spooky or malevolent. I have not differentiated between verified and unverified sightings in this chapter, as I am focusing on children's impressions, and the meaning of the experience is the main significance to the child, and sometimes the parent.

## Child ghosts in the home

Domestic ghosts are the most frequently reported sightings, especially child ghosts – these seem to have a natural affinity with living children. Most are seen in the child's bedroom, partly because ghosts are most readily perceived after dark or in the early morning when the child is quiet and relaxed. The first experience I have described is perhaps the most typical kind of childhood ghost encounter – the presence was verified but not until years later. I met Nicky at an Enchanted Fairy evening I organised on the Isle of Wight, England. Nicky told me:

> When I was young, I had an invisible dog called Whisky, black and white with fluffy fur. I would answer the front door to let it in. It stopped coming after two years.
>
> Then Simon came. I woke up in the night feeling vibrations. He was sitting on my doll's cot wearing little shorts and a blue cotton top and shoes with buckles. He looked like a real person, but his form illuminated the room with light. I was not frightened. We

looked at each other, and he said 'What's your name?' I told him it was Nicola. I asked him what he was called and he said he was Simon. I knew he was friendly. The doll's cot was in the middle of the two beds in my room. Philip, my mother's friend's little boy, was sleeping in the next bed, but by the time I woke him Simon had disappeared.

Many years later I was taking a course at the Arthur Findlay College for Spiritual Studies and one of the mediums who was working with us told me there was a little boy beside me who had revealed himself only to me. He was really excited to be there. The doll's cot was by now in my own daughter Lois's room but was not played with. When I got home Verity, my other daughter, said she was sorry but a panel had come off the cot. So for me that was evidence that I really had seen Simon as a child.

If a child sees a ghost, it is often hard for him or her to confide in sceptical adults, especially if the ghost is an unfamiliar figure. However, for many children the experience is special and seems to give them a quiet assurance. The late Vivien Greene, who was married to the writer Graham Greene, told me that she saw her phantom child when she was six.

My father, Sidney B Browning, was a manager in the British American Tobacco Company. It meant that my family – my mother, my younger brother and myself – were always being moved from place to place, and even when very small I hated these constant moves.

It was in winter, probably December, one evening, and I was standing in front of the stairs. The staircase was on my left. A narrow passage ran down in front of me to what I think was the back door. A sitting room door was on my right. Suddenly the door and the wall at the end of the passage disappeared and I saw the dark-blue night sky with glittering stars in the winter sky. Between me and the air, but nearer where the door had been, stood a child of about my own age, naked, perfectly solid in appearance and colour, with the extraordinary addition, in which I was much interested and noticed more than anything else, of white silk openwork socks, what I thought of as party socks.

We looked at each other, and my mother called out from the sitting room, 'Finn, there's a terrible draught. Do shut the door,' or words to that effect, whether in French – Finn was the cook – or English I do not know. Instantly the apparition vanished and the wall and the door were as normal. I did not speak of this for at least ten years and felt even then very reluctant to mention it. It was a rather sacred and holy experience, and I still think of it with much awe and wonder.

The date would have been 1910 or 1911.

Vivien did not discover the identity of her apparition.

## Adult ghosts

Children may also encounter an adult figure, and this can be more worrying for them. Unless the experience is sensitively handled, a child may become afraid of burglars or intruders.

Anne, who lives in Sussex, England, describes her experience:

When I was about six years old I woke one bright sunny morning to see someone standing in front of my chest of drawers in front of the windows. I slept in a large room with my nanny and my little brother. Thinking this person was Nanny, I called to her. The figure turned, walked towards my bed and bent over me. He was a tall elegant gentleman with a long coat with brass buttons and a fur collar, I think astrakhan. He carried a walking cane with a silver top, a pair of gloves and no hat. He was smoky grey and transparent, but the buttons and the top of the walking cane shone. I was terrified and shot under the bedclothes.

After a short while, curiosity got the better of me, and I peeped out to find he had moved to the bottom of the bed and, horror of horrors, was melting. Thankfully, in a short space of time he did. I never told anyone, but about a year or two later we left that house and went to a brand-new one. I then told my mother, who was, of course, very upset that I had been so frightened and not told anyone. She explained about spirit people, and since then I have never been in the least afraid.

Later in life, in my teens, I had poltergeist experiences. This can be alarming, especially when they jump on top of you when you are in bed. I managed to get to the light switch and the light drove it off.

June, who lives in Oxfordshire, England, told me the story of her father, Oscar, who was born in India in 1877, the eldest child of an army chaplain.

The family did not have much money, and Oscar's wealthy Uncle Howard in England offered to educate Oscar on condition that he could adopt the child, who would take his name. Oscar's father's reaction was 'Aren't we lucky?', but his mother was in tears. However, his father pointed out that they would not see Oscar for many years anyway, as he would have to be sent to England for his education. Oscar, his mother and the three younger children travelled to England. Then, on the appointed day, dressed in his Eton suit for the first time, Oscar took the train with his mother to Hastings, where they were to meet Uncle Howard for lunch at the hotel where he lived.

Throughout the meal, Oscar kept asking, 'Who are the men in the garden? Why are they wearing funny clothes?' Annoyed, Uncle Howard sent for the gardener, who said there was no one in the garden. Both the gardener and the waiter gave Oscar a funny look.

Furious, Uncle Howard said that he was not taking on a boy who told lies. As they were leaving the hotel, the waiter came up to Oscar's mother and said, 'Don't worry. He's got the sight. My father worked here before me, and there were prisoners of the Napoleonic wars tied against the wall. The clothes would have been like the boy described.

The unexpected sight of the ghosts, although they may have made Oscar appear a liar in his uncle's eyes, saved him from a potentially disastrous relationship with a man obviously unsympathetic to children. Instead, Oscar's mother and the four children stayed in Oxford, where he went to school and the family lived – on limited means, since there were two households to maintain, but they were very happy.

## Sharing the vision

It sometimes happens that a mother or father sees a ghost at the same time that their child does. This can be reassuring if the parent does not panic, though some parents deny the experience to try to spare the child being afraid. This can, as I have discovered from the numerous interviews I have carried out, actually isolate the child, causing them much anxiety and leaving them alone with fears that are very real and yet not acknowledged.

Amanda, who works at a hotel near Swindon in Wiltshire, England, told me about the little boy ghost who shared her childhood home:

> When I was very young we moved to an old house in Ruabon that used to be a school. Frequently the hall door would bang open when no one was around and there was no wind. Someone used to blow down my ear, and I would see strange white mists in the corner. I knew – I'm not sure how – that there was a young boy around. I was never afraid, as it was a friendly presence, just part of life – one of the family really. I grew up with him and accepted him.
>
> My dad laughed and told me it was imagination. However, when I was about eight, the ghost appeared to my dad: a young boy wearing a long white nightshirt. It frightened the life out of him, and he never laughed again when I told him the little boy was there. We were at the house 12 years, and the little boy stayed around the whole time.
>
> Once I was eavesdropping and heard the neighbours talking about our ghost. The previous owner, an old lady, had never heard or seen him but he was legendary to the house. I wondered if, as I was a child, the little ghost was attracted by my toys.

He may, of course, have been a pupil who died at the school many years before.

Belinda, an actress and writer living in London, England, also saw a ghost at a school when she was a child, but it was not until she was an adult that she discovered her experience was more than the product of a lively imagination. She told me:

I was so ill with asthma when I was a child that I was sent to a boarding school for asthmatics. I saw my ghost when I was eight years old. I was in bed and woke to see a boy sitting at the end of my bed, smiling at me. There was an elderly man sitting in an armchair behind the boy. In reality, the armchair did not exist, as I was in a four-bed girls' dormitory. I sat up, and the boy kept smiling. I realised that he was not a boy who went to the school. I screamed and screamed and ran into the bathroom next door, waking up the entire school (20 or so children) as well as the headmistress, who was on night duty and therefore sleeping in the duty room. She came into the bathroom and calmed me down, telling me that there was no boy in the room.

Years later, when I was in my twenties, I met my former headmistress and reminded her about the incident. She told me what she could not say at the time, that a young boy had died in my dormitory two years before. I had seen the apparition. She showed me a photograph of the school children when the boy had attended, and I pointed to the boy who appeared to me. She then confirmed that this was the boy who died not long after the photograph had been taken and appeared to me two years later. She had been aware that I had seen his ghost.

A few years ago, I visited the school and was shown around by a female teacher. I mentioned my experience, and she confirmed that there had been sightings of the boy but that the headmaster refused to hear about such nonsense and so everything was kept quiet.

Who was the old man? Perhaps an elderly housemaster who tended his sick charges during the night. It may be that the presence of the first ghost elicited that of the second or that they were from different times but had the school as a binding force. As with many childhood experiences, the adult involved did not admit to Belinda – out of the best motives – that she had seen a ghost.

In Beverley's case, her mother also saw the ghosts in their home, though it was not till many years later that she admitted it. Beverley remembers:

I woke in the middle of the night to find several human figures floating past the bed. The figures were like sharp shadows, black in silhouette, but not against a wall – rather like black cardboard cut-outs in profile. There were several, but I was most aware of a portly gentleman who passed by. The image was so sharp that I can recall the outline of the waistcoat buttons and cutaway coats.

As they went out of the door, I seemed to lose sight of them. I called out to my mother, who came into the room. She didn't acknowledge them at the time. She later told me she hadn't wanted to frighten me. I remember saying, 'One's just gone right through you.'

At the time, Beverley lived very close to a traditionally Quaker area. In later life she has been drawn towards Quakerism, though she has not actually become a Quaker.

Beverley's mother, Joy, recalls the incident. She says that she told Beverley she was dreaming, because she did not want to worry her.

> I remember it very clearly. I wish I had written the date down in my diary, but at the time I was more anxious to gloss the incident over, although strangely it was not at all frightening. But I thought at the time Beverley might have been worried. On this particular night she called out, and I got out of bed and went to her bedroom, which was next to ours. On reaching the door, I was startled to see these groups of figures standing just inside the door.
>
> As Beverley said, they were a small group of dark figures, very plain but the faces were not clear. They appeared to be wearing cloaks and had tall hats that led us to believe they might be Quakers.
>
> I moved forwards, and suddenly they glided towards the end of the room and disappeared. We did both notice that one of the figures was shorter than the others.

Gloria who lives in East Yorkshire, England, wrote:

> A few years ago I was visiting friends who lived in an old rectory. My four-year-old granddaughter, Georgina, was with me. As I escorted her slowly down the large staircase, I suddenly saw an elderly, white-haired lady standing at the foot of the stairs. She was dressed in black and was smiling at me. At that point my granddaughter stumbled, and I bent down to steady her. When I looked down, the old lady was no longer there.
>
> Reaching the bottom of the stairs, little Georgina looked around then asked me: 'Where has the nice lady gone, Nana?'
>
> My friends assured me that no one else was in the house and they had no idea who the lady was. If it had not been for my granddaughter's question, I would simply have dismissed the appearance as a trick of my imagination. My friends delved into the previous owners of their old rectory, but no haunting came to light.

The ghost seen by Lloyd, whose mother, Leigh, contacted me from the Isle of Wight, England, is the strangest I have encountered, because it was very much like the traditional ghost in a white sheet. The white sheet was originally, no doubt, a way of describing the white mist, or etheric light, perceived around some ghosts as they materialise. Leigh told me:

> Three years ago my son saw a white figure outside the glass doors downstairs. According to Lloyd, he seemed to be dressed in a white sheet or blanket, like a fictional or cartoon ghost such as Casper.

> Then, six months later, my son and I saw both saw it outside the upstairs window. I asked if this was what he had seen before, and he said yes. We both watched the figure outside the window, so strange, as if someone had put a white sheet over themselves.
>
> It became denser and denser and then disappeared like mist. We live near an old priory – about two minutes' walk away.

Because Leigh accepted the truth of her son's story even before she had seen the ghost herself, her son was also able to accept the experience and not give it undue importance in his life. If ghosts are just regarded as a natural phenomenon and not as a big deal, then the child is able to remain focused on the everyday world.

## Grandparents who return

Not surprisingly, a grandparent who has been involved in a child's life may return after their death to see the child, and sometimes becomes a guardian to the child. I am convinced that love survives beyond the grave, and a child will usually accept a ghostly grandparent quite happily. Such an apparition can also be reassuring for a parent who is struggling with personal grief and feels that they can no longer sense the love of the deceased family member.

Rosanne, who lives in Shropshire, England, was very supportive of her son Nicklas when he started to see her late father. Nicklas's grandfather died when the boy was three years old, and it was not until he was he was six that he started to talk about his 'guard' – his name for his grandfather. Rosanne told me:

> Sometimes Nicklas would go into a corner and start talking to his grandfather, who seemed to act as his guardian angel.

Then Rosanne's car was stolen.

> Nicklas came to me in the garden and said that his guard knew where the car was. He kept going across the lawn and apparently talking into thin air, listening and then coming back to me. He said there were two bridges and the car was by the first bridge. There were a lot of shops not far away, and sometimes we went to the place for a picnic, and there was a special church I had been to. When I suggested several places, Nicklas got annoyed and said it was where cars went over and under the bridges. I put it down to an over-active imagination.
>
> When the car was found, it was on a slip road just off a dual carriageway. There were two bridges nearby. The car was by the first bridge. A couple of miles back were Telford shopping centre and the park, where we had had a couple of picnics. Not far to the right of the place was the Spiritualist church that I had attended a couple of times since my father died. But how did Nicklas know?

Verification can occur when the child reports from the visiting ghostly grandparent information that the family did not know.

Mary, who lives in County Wicklow, Ireland, described how her late husband came back to see his granddaughter.

> When my granddaughter, Marie, was three years old, she told my daughter, Sian, that she had been talking to Grampy. She said that Grampy looked young but had told her that there were no pubs in heaven. Grampy was wearing his pyjamas.
>
> On Grampy's next visit, Marie reported that he was wearing his shirt and trousers. Sian was pregnant, and Grampy told Marie that Mummy would have the new baby very soon. He sent the message, 'You must not be disappointed that the baby is a girl again.'
>
> Everybody was expecting a boy. It was Sian's third baby after two girls, and the baby was a completely different shape in the womb. Sian had been calling him Shannon and buying blue things. Marie reported that Grampy said the family could still call the girl Shannon, as it was a good Irish name. Soon after this conversation, Sian went into labour, and the baby was a girl. She was called Shannon.

Grampy did not visit Marie again until just before Sian's fourth baby was due. This time he assured Marie that she was going to have a brother and that it would be coming straight away. The baby was born, as predicted, very shortly after Grampy's visit, a boy.

Occasionally, a grandparent will use a sound to alert a grandchild so as not to alarm them. Diane, from Suffolk, England, told me:

> It had not been long since my grandfather passed away when some unexplicable things happened. He was the most important man in my life, someone I had complete respect for, and I looked up to him. It was a dreadful shock losing him when I was so young. Suddenly, at only 14 years old, I had to come to terms with losing a very special friend.
>
> I can vividly remember waking up in the middle of the night to the sound of my musical box playing. At first I thought I was dreaming and that the music would soon stop, but it did not. I got out of bed and walked to the dressing table. The musical box had the lid securely shut. I realised at once something was strange, as the music only started when the box was open, so that the ballerina could dance round to the music. I can remember feeling very nervous when I lifted the box up to try to stop the music. I opened the lid as usual, and everything was in place. The ballerina circled round, but I could not stop the music. The music did not stop till I removed the musical component.
>
> A few nights later, I woke up again in the night and I knew I had to walk towards the stairs. There I saw an image of my

grandfather as a light reflection, though there was no light penetrating the curtains. I was wide awake.

## Returning grandparents who are not known to the child

Some children are too young to recall the grandparent, who may even have died years before they were born, but can accurately describe them, despite never having seen a photo.

Hannah, who lives in Ayrshire, Scotland, never met her paternal grandmother, but the grandmother still became a guardian to her, even in adult life.

From when I was very young, I saw things and heard things. My father's mother died when he was 22, and we had no photos of her. I had never seen her. When I was nine years old, I woke one night, worried about exams and a project that I had to do for school. A lady, about five foot two [154 centimetres], wearing old-fashioned clothes, was standing behind the door. She was very real and solid but was dark-skinned and dark-eyed, whereas our family was mainly very fair and blue-eyed. She told me that I was not to worry and that everything would be fine, as she would look after me because she was my grandmother. I was not at all afraid, because there was wonderful warmth in the room. My exams went well, as did my project, and I had a sense of being cared for and protected from beyond.

When I was 16, I saw a photograph of my grandmother for the first time, and it was the lady I had seen all those years ago, dark-skinned and with dark eyes, wearing clothes similar to those in which I had seen her all those years before. I became quite tearful when I saw the picture.

Lyndsey, who lives in Swansea, Wales, told me:

When I was about seven years old, I had a dream about a man in a green army suit. He took my hand and led me into a most beautiful garden surrounded by flowers. I still remember the dream as if it happened only yesterday. He kept handing me bunches of flowers, and it seemed as though we were there for hours and we talked and talked.

The next day I couldn't stop thinking about the man in the green army suit, so I told my mother, and her face just dropped. She asked me to look at a photo. The person in the photo and my dream was my granddad. But I did not know anything about him. I didn't even know I had a grandfather until the day after my dream. I was really spooked by this. I kept thinking, how could I dream about him if I had never seen or known him?

My mum then explained that he died when she was a young girl. He was in the RAF and he had been crushed by machinery. He was taken to hospital, but there was nothing they could do for him. I have found out a lot about him in the last few years from my grandmother and photos that she has. Everyone thinks I look very much like him, as I have his features and speech hesitation.

My mum believes he wanted to visit me and he did so through my dream. Now I often dream about him and feel close to him, but I do not know why.

In the case of Sadie, who lives in Yorkshire, England, her son, Lewis, formed a bond with a great-grandma who had seen him only once, as an infant, before she died. Lewis had not seen any photographs.

My newborn son, Lewis, yawned as his great-grandma held him and commented on what a bonny baby he was. My husband, Glen, who was 24, and I had taken the baby to show Glen's grandparents, Jayne and David, for the first time. Jayne only saw Lewis once more before she died.

We continued to visit Glen's grandfather regularly. One Sunday when Lewis was four, we went round. Lewis was playing on the living room floor. 'Where's that lady gone?' he asked suddenly. 'There was a lady with dark hair sitting there.' He was staring at the chair where Glen's grandmother always sat. When we got home, we asked him about the lady. 'She had dark curly hair, big glasses and a mark on her neck,' he told us. Jayne had worn big glasses, had dark curly hair and a dark mole that was very noticeable on her neck. 'She had her hands out like this,' said Lewis, putting out his hands in the way his great-grandmother had cradled him as an infant. Lewis had never seen a photograph of Jayne. Those that existed were in family albums he had never been shown.

That Christmas we went to see Glen's grandfather. His Aunt Sylvia came with us. We did not say anything at the time but afterwards asked Lewis if he had seen the lady in the chair. 'Yes,' he said, 'but she was upstairs watching Aunty Sylvia was doing things properly.' Sylvia was the eldest daughter. Her mother had been very house-proud.

Our young daughter has seen nothing on the visits.

Angela, who lives on the Isle of Wight, England, was frightened when her son started talking about his great-grandfather's presence. She told me:

My son's name is Reice. He saw my grandfather, whose name was Laurence, when he was about two years old. Reice had got into bed with me, and as I was just getting comfy, he piped up: 'Man's here.'

I asked him whom he was talking about, and Reice replied: 'He's very tall and he's got white hair and has got a hat on.' Although this was a basic description, it sounded like my grandfather. Reice then said, 'He's a very nice man.'

By now I was getting a bit spooked, so I asked Reice to tell the man to go away, which he did. His eyes then followed something leaving the room. Opposite my bedroom is the bathroom, and the light for it is on the wall outside. Just as Reice looked out of the door, the bathroom light switched on. I said to Reice, 'Tell the man to go away.' He told me not to worry because it was just Granddad. I got up and switched off the bathroom light and Reice said, 'He's gone now.'

## Foretelling the death

I have encountered a number of cases in which a young child informs the rest of the family that a grandparent or great-grandparent has died, even when the family has no contact. The grandparent seems to visit the child around the point of death, perhaps because they know that the child will be the most welcoming and receptive family member.

Layla, now a clairvoyant herself, was only 21 months old when she saw her great-grandfather, whom the family called Granddad Bert. Layla's mother, Carla, who lives in Cheshire, England, told me that she and the children hardly ever saw Granddad Bert. He was an overbearing man at the best of times, and when he developed senile dementia, his behaviour became so problematic that Carla could not face taking the children to see him.

He died unexpectedly at about 4 am on a Wednesday morning but, since the family had lost touch with him, Carla was not told about the death. Carla says:

At about 11 in the morning Layla stopped playing in the living room and looked up as if she was looking into someone's face. 'It's Granddad Bert,' she said. She ran to where, apparently, he was standing, looked up into his face and then shrugged as if to say, 'He's gone.' Then she ran back and carried on playing.

I thought this was odd, as we never saw Granddad Bert, so when my husband came home about 4 pm, I said: 'I suppose we'd better see if he's all right.' My husband rang his mum, and she said that Granddad Bert had died early that morning.

Three-year-old Kenny, who lived in Bournemouth, England, didn't know his Great-uncle Clancy, in Ireland. His grandma told me this story.

One afternoon Kenny said to his nan: 'I've just seen Clan-Clan. He came to tell me he's dead but he's all right.' Clan-Clan was Uncle Clancy's pet name, used when he was a child by his mum. Uncle Clancy had been ill for some time, but there hadn't been any recent news, as the family wasn't in close touch. Soon afterwards, the message came of Clancy's death.

A couple of years later, Kenny stopped and looked and said, 'Oh, Clan-Clan,' but would say no more.

Diane, from Liverpool, England, described how her son reported on the demise of an elderly great-aunt:

> When my eldest son was three years old, he was playing in his bedroom. I went in to check on him, and he said to me: 'I've just seen Auntie Louie. She was in my bedroom.'
>
> The house we were living in at the time was the house that my father-in-law's family grew up in, and Aunt Louie, as everyone called her, was my father-in-law's sister. He had passed away some years back. I felt a bit spooked by what my son had said, because we never really had anything to do with the old aunts and uncles, and we didn't even know at the time that she had passed away. It was some weeks later that we found out she had died.
>
> Then something else that was strange happened. My brother and his wife came to visit us, and I was telling them the ghost story. As I was explaining, I was pouring us all a cup of tea. When I passed a cup to my sister-in-law, the cup exploded in a thousand pieces, leaving us all spooked. Then, about 12 months later, my son mentioned that he had seen Aunt Louie again.

## Coming to terms with a sibling's death

When a child dies, the parents' grief is unimaginable, but often it can be as hard for a sibling, who not only suddenly loses a playmate but may also fear that they too are going to die. However, I have come across numerous cases in which a young child has seen and played with a deceased sibling. The deceased child usually stays around for as long as they are needed. Often, such appearances reassure a parent, who may be unable to connect with the dead child themselves because of overwhelming sorrow. Although the matter-of-fact nature of these encounters is generally very comforting, it can be difficult for the living child if outsiders laugh at or dismiss their experience. In one case I know of, a teacher pushed a little girl out of the room and shut the door when she tried to tell the teacher about playing with a dead brother. I am sure this was due not to unkindness but to the teacher being at a complete loss about how to deal with the matter. Because the paranormal is pushed under the carpet by education and health professionals, a valuable therapeutic tool is lost for a grieving child, whether the experience is imagination or not. Psychic experiences do not delay healing, and they cease when the child is ready to move on.

Calum died of leukaemia in hospital when he was four, and his mother, Jan, had reassuring dreams of her son. However, it was his sister, Jade, who actually saw Calum after his death. Jan, who lives in Southampton, England, says:

> Jade told me that she often played with her brother after his death. One morning, some months later, she told me: 'Calum came

into my bedroom last night. He's really strong now, Mummy, stronger than when he was alive.'

Then one day Jade was sitting colouring a picture of a turtle when she told me, quite matter-of-factly: 'Calum doesn't need me any more now. He's really happy now.'

Two years after my initial conversation with Jan, I met her again, pushing a pram containing a beautiful baby girl. She told me that Jade had seen Calum once more:

She came rushing home from school and told her mother, 'Calum was in assembly with me. The girl next to me couldn't see him, but I moved over to give him space.'

'What was he wearing?' Jan asked.

'Oh, not exactly purple, lilac-coloured shorts and a top in lilac patterns with a hood.'

Just before Calum died, Jan had bought him a new lilac top and shorts. When he died she had pulled them from the top of his suitcase and put them on Calum for the funeral. Jade had never seen the clothes, and Jan hadn't talked about them to anyone.

'What was he wearing on his feet?' Jan asked.

'I couldn't see because he was flying.'

Robbie also died of leukaemia, when he was 11. Three days after his death, his mother, Margaret, from Berkshire, saw Robbie in his bedroom. He was wearing what the family used to jokingly call his Rupert Bear trousers. He was getting something off the top of his tallboy, where he kept all his treasures. Robbie had grown. In life, the radium treatment had stopped his spine growing, so his legs had grown but not his body. Now, in the vision, he appeared to have grown normally. He smiled at his mother, who was so shocked she burst into tears and ran away. She did not tell Lindsey, Robbie's four-year-old sister, about this incident.

However, Lindsey saw Robbie after death herself. She was nearly 14 when I last spoke to her, but could still remember Robbie coming back to see her. She told me:

Before he died, Robbie was always organising games for us. He was great fun. Sometimes we would play schools, and he would be the teacher. He was always making me laugh.

At one time, at the old house, after Robbie died, the girl next door used to take my best friends away to her house, so I would be left with no one to play with. I would be wandering round the house with nothing to do. If I was by myself, Robbie would usually turn up. I would talk to him and play with him. He still used to make me laugh.

When I was six or seven and we had moved to our new house, I went into my friend Nick's sitting room. Nick said, 'I'll get my new train set,' and disappeared upstairs. I heard someone coming downstairs a few minutes afterwards. I thought it was Nicky and I said, 'Hurry up.'

'When I looked round, it was Robbie sitting next to me. I told Nick, but he made fun of me and told my mum, 'Guess what Lindsey said she saw at my house!'

Luckily Lindsey's mother reassured her that the sighting was normal and was a very special sign of love. Robbie stopped coming when Lindsey no longer needed him.

## Frightening ghosts

Some children are scared by the ghosts they see, either because – as with living people – they instinctively know the ghost is not nice or because the setting of the encounter is unsettling. Such experiences need a great deal of telling and retelling to the parent, and reassurance that the ghost is just an apparition, like a scary film on television, and cannot hurt them. I discuss this further in Chapter 9, starting on page 141.

Nikki explained how, when she was a child, she saw some ghosts in the mirror. There are various ancient superstitions about souls being trapped in a mirror, and a similar experience is described by Adela on page 166. I am not sure why these mirror experiences are so frightening for children. It may be that the ghost seems more sinister because it is a reflection where the child's own image should be. The mirror is a tool used by clairvoyants to see pictures of the future or past, and the child may be experiencing in some way a rush of psychic power they do not understand. Nikki says:

We were living in a council house in Hertfordshire, and I was not very old. In our second bedroom there was an oval mirror on the dressing table, and I would often look in the mirror. Once, I glanced in the mirror and saw a little girl and boy on a seesaw. It was cloudy and misty, but I could see the background. They were playing. There were trees and sky in the mirror, and the seesaw was set in a lump of concrete.

They looked at me. There was a sense of everything slowing down in the body and then a weird sense of everything so fast I could feel my body swell. My lips felt as if they had swollen up, and I was not in control.

For Andrea, who lives in Portsmouth, England, it was the sinister appearance of the ghost that spooked her.

When I was eight years old I saw a ghost in our house. It was not till years later that I found out my brother had seen the figure too. He described in detail what he had seen, and I realised it was the same man. It was strange we never told each other.

The ghost seemed an ordinary enough man, like lots of others round our way, except for the fact that he wore gangster-type clothing, a dark-brown double-breasted coat, long and belted at the waist, and a big Al Capone-type hat pulled over his eyes.

Several years later we moved to another part of Portsmouth and met a couple who used to live near our old house but had moved away years before. As we got chatting, it turned out that the woman's family had lived in the house next to my old one for years before we'd lived there. She said our house had a bit of a reputation in the old days. The man who had lived in our old house in the 1930s had committed suicide. Her mother always said he used to dress up in gangster-type clothes, which had shocked the neighbours, because it was a very respectable area.

Patricia, who lives in Kent, England, was also scared because the figure she saw in her home one night was unusual, though in no way malevolent. When she was 12, she saw the ghost of a woman with a big shawl, a Spanish comb in her hair and rings on her fingers. The woman was about 75.

I was very scared when I saw her, and she vanished when I spoke. I told Mum, but she told me not to be silly and to go back to bed. I had six brothers and sisters, and she said I must not frighten them.

When she left her parents' room, however, Patricia stayed listening on the stairs. She heard her mum say to her dad: 'Pat's just seen Old Mother Moore.' This woman had died while living over the shop that Pat's parents now owned.

Pauline lives in Australia, but she grew up in Scotland. Her psychic experience terrified her, because she was locked in a dark cellar and could not escape from the apparitions. The incident occurred near what is now one of the most popular ghost walks in Edinburgh. The ghosts were not malevolent, and it appears they were actually trying to comfort the frightened child.

As a child of four years old, I often went in the evenings to help my granny, who worked as a cleaner in the Royal Bank, in Tron Square in Edinburgh.

These excursions were often spoiled by fear and anxiety. When asked to take the huge wastepaper sack down to the cellar, I would always plead that my sister Shelagh should help me because it was too heavy. Really it was to make sure I was never on my own down in the cellars. Children are quick to discover the weaknesses of others, and my sister was no exception. Helping me down, she would run back up the stairs first, often switching off the light.

The cellars of the bank were reached by plain stone stairs and a wide barren passageway, and were massive and cavern-like. Off this main corridor was another corridor, of which, for as long as I can remember, I had had a dread.

Granny's niece, Kathleen, was ten years old, and one night decided to help Granny with us. I was five years old and a bit scared of this big girl. As the night wore on and Kathleen and I went down to the cellar to empty wastepaper bins into the big sack, we seemed to be getting on fine. As she was so much older than I was and knew where everything was, I followed her like a puppy.

At the end of the long passage, a huge door blocked the way. Kathleen found a key for the padlock. Very soon we were inside what I discovered was the coal cellar. She showed me where the coal was dropped from the pavement above, through huge metal doors with massive bars across them. I was intrigued by this and remembered Granny telling me that the coalman came every Thursday and that she got the place ready for each new lot of coal.

What I was not ready for was the door closing with a slam and the light outside being turned off, leaving me standing in complete darkness, unable to move with fright. All I could hear was Kathleen giggling and running away. I ran to the door, falling over coal on the way, screaming and banging on the door for ages, crying at the same time. I soon realised that no one could hear me and stopped crying for a moment, in the hope that Granny would come and get me out.

What I did hear was something quite different. It was sniffling and weeping, coming from the huge, high coal area. I turned round slowly, staring at what was behind me. Paralysed with fear and not knowing what to do, I beheld a crowd of people sitting on the coal, the stark black only highlighting the pale outlines, in dim white. Mothers with babies, men and women holding each other in pain and fear, and lots of old people. All came towards me as if trying to tell me something. I felt them say, 'Don't be afraid. Do not cry.' But that only made me feel worse. Within a few moments they were right beside me, reaching out as if to comfort me. I was petrified. Then, after what seemed an eternity, the light in the corridor went on. Granny was shouting at Kathleen.

Granny opened the great doors and I was free, crying and sobbing and telling her what I had seen. She said: 'They'll no harm you, lassie. They're just poor souls trying to help you.'

Not until the late seventies did it become known that Edinburgh's Royal Mile was built directly on an older city and that plague had wiped out many of the previous inhabitants.

Plague broke out in the warren of closes, shops and booths beneath the Royal Mile in December 1645 and raged through the old town until early 1646, and the new town was built on top of the old. Pauline had seen some of the plague victims.

## Psychic touch and ghosts

I mentioned at the beginning of the chapter that children are often gifted at picking up images of the past from old artefacts simply by touching them. This art is called psychometry and seems to work via the *chakras,* or psychic energy centres, that we have in the palms of our hands. When Linda was a child, living in north Florida, she handled some artefacts belonging to a friend's ancestor and automatically linked with the person they belonged to. Linda reported:

> When I was 12 I went to stay with my friend, Felicity. The house was a modern single-storey one, built in the 1960s, and I had stayed there before. On this occasion, Hilary showed me some treasures from the American Civil War that had belonged to her great-great-grandmother, Octavia Stevens. Octavia had been married to an officer who had fought for the South. Although there had not been a lot of action in Florida, there was a big battle that turned into a massacre with bayonets and no prisoners were taken.
>
> The old family house was to be sold, and Octavia's diaries, pictures and artefacts were being donated to a museum. They were spread around the living room. My friend also took me to see Octavia's husband's sword, which was in the garage. It was so huge and heavy that you could hardly lift it.
>
> That night, I was lying in bed and could not get to sleep properly in a strange place. Felicity had made a bed on the floor for herself and was fast asleep. As I looked across the hallway, I saw a woman walk from the living room to the bathroom. I heard a rustling noise like satin skirts and a humming like a hair dryer. The woman wore a white robe. She looked to neither the right nor the left.
>
> I saw her quite clearly. I was terrified and tried to make sense of the experience, as I felt total disbelief. Could it have been Felicity's mother, even though the woman looked nothing like her? About an hour later, there was an almighty crash from the bathroom as the entire shelving unit fell down.
>
> I told my friend's mother what had happened, and she did not laugh at me but was very concerned that I should not be upset. She had not visited the bedroom during the night but seemed to know whom I had seen.

Many years later, when I was living in England, my mother sent me a cutting about the collection of Octavia's treasures, including all her letters, which was housed in a museum in northern Florida. I believe Octavia was disturbed that her treasures were being moved and came back to show her displeasure to the family.

## When a child sees a ghost

If a child tells you they have seen a strange figure that disappeared into mist, accept the experience as you would any other. Without expressing fear or disbelief, allow them to recount it, and then ask if they want to know anything. This may be an opportunity for the child to bring up issues about death, especially if they know of someone who has recently died.

It is less important to try to verify the experience than to help the child not to feel odd or spooked, but rather to think that they have seen something special and so were very lucky. The experience was real to the child and so should not be dismissed as imagination, especially if the child can see something you do not.

If you do see or sense the ghost yourself, then say so, but do not make any big deal about it. You can wish the ghost goodbye and say, 'Thank you for appearing to us. We wish you well. Go in peace.' If the child is frightened, explain that they are seeing pictures from the past that cannot harm them.

Reassure the child that they will probably not see a ghost again, but devise rituals in case the child does, so they stay in control. For example, you could buy a crystal angel that the child can keep by the bed to hold, or you could devise a special prayer the child can say before bed and if they feel worried during the night. Soft lighting may be helpful in dark corners. Your child may want to rearrange the bedroom or swap rooms.

Don't rush your child off to see a psychologist for – as you can see from this chapter – encounters with ghosts are common, even though they are rarely spoken of. For this reason, suggest to your child that they talk of the experience only within the home, not because there is anything to be ashamed of but because, sadly, educational and health professionals may react negatively through ignorance and their own fears. Explain also that other children may tease them, even though they may themselves have had similar experiences.

Make sure the child has plenty of earthly stimulation and that their television viewing is kept very bland for a while after the experience. Teenagers especially may need a mixture of common sense and sensitive input, particularly if they have been watching scary films at friends' houses (more about this on page 155).

If you want to research a ghost your child saw, ask elderly neighbours or visit a local library or record office and you may discover someone answering to the name or description the child gave. If you do not find anything, it does not mean the ghost was not real. It may well have belonged to a former house on the spot centuries before.

## How to deal with the issue of death

Seeing a beloved grandparent after death can be a reassurance that love does continue. Even if you do not believe in any form of afterlife, accept that this experience is one way of expressing the concept that love and fond memories do not die.

Explain to the child that some people do believe that after a person's body dies, the real person inside goes to heaven or an afterlife and that the grandparent may occasionally want to watch over them like a guardian angel. However, this is likely to be just an occasional visit, like one from a distant relative overseas. Reassure your child that the grandparent loves them and would never frighten them.

Encourage your child to express grief for the deceased family member and let them see that you are also sad. Explain to them that it is right to be sad. Because modern society expects people to be back at work within a short time of bereavement, feelings can get buried and can come out as negative ghost encounters for a child.

Encourage the child to help you make up a family memory box containing small treasures belonging to close relatives who have died. Even if the child does not know the ghostly grandparent, they can then see that the person did once live on earth and was quite ordinary.

# CHAPTER 3

# Children Who See into the Future

Throughout history, children have been regarded as seers and used by adults to predict future events. In ancient Greece, young boys would gaze into bowls of pure water lit by burning torches to see what was going to happen in the state.

Paracelsus, the sixteenth-century philosopher, physician and alchemist, recommended as prophets young boys and girls born out of wedlock (presumably because they were not, at that time, brought up by parents). These children were considered to be in a state of innocence and so possessing unclouded psychic vision. Incense and perfumes were burned around the child prophet, and their brow, thought to be the seat of the clairvoyant eye, was anointed with sacred oils such as frankincense and sandalwood. Prayers were said to invoke the Archangels, and the child was given a crystal sphere to hold. Gradually, the mists would clear and a vision appear within the glass.

Children also used the Theurgic Mirror. This was a bottle of clear water. The child would ask questions and the Archangel Gabriel would show them pictures in the water to give the answers.

Similarly, Cagliostro, the eighteenth-century magician, used young children to help him predict the future. Often, these would be children from educated families chosen for training because of their psychic gifts. In one reported incident, the five-year-old son of Marshal von Medem saw the unexpected arrival home of his elder brother and was able to describe what was going on in other rooms of the house. He was using the Mirror of Cagliostro, a bottle of clear water, set on a piece of furniture. The child stood gazing into the water. Cagliostro placed his hands on the child's head and told him the questions to ask. The answers would appear as actual pictures of people and places or as symbols.

### How can seeing into the future be possible?

Clock time is relative. When I talk to my publisher in Los Angeles at teatime in England, she is just getting into the office at 8 am. When the Gregorian calendar was introduced into mainland Europe in 1582, 11 days vanished from the calendar. However, the new calendar was not adopted in Protestant England until 1752. So what happened to the lost days?

It has been hypothesised that the right side of the brain, from which the imagination emanates, is the hemisphere where prophetic abilities may exist, and by using the right brain, people can tap into future possibilities. The left side of the brain is concerned with organising present and past experience. Once a child becomes aware of measured time and the left side of their brain becomes more developed, the child becomes more ruled by the limitations of clock time. Though seeing into the future is not as prevalent among children as telepathy, nevertheless I have come across a significant number of incidents, especially where strong emotions such as a sense of danger to a family member are involved.

## Warnings of danger to loved ones

Just as mothers seem to have automatic radar that can anticipate danger to their children, so a young child who is with their mother may become aware when danger is near. Elspeth, a former accountant living on the south coast of England, can recall, more than 50 years later, how her premonition saved her mother's life.

> During the Second World War, when I was five, my family were living in Portland. Dad was in the Merchant Navy – he was a salvage diver – and my mother decided that we would stay where he was based so we wouldn't be separated.
>
> Mum and I were walking along the beach with our red setter Blue. I can remember him now. 'Quick, Mum!' I suddenly shouted. 'There's a bad plane coming.'
>
> 'No, there isn't, love,' she reassured me, looking up at the sky. But I grabbed her and called the dog, and we ran behind a rock. Mum went along with my warning to humour me. Seconds later a bomber dropped a bomb on the beach a bit ahead of where we were walking. The water sprayed over us. I hadn't heard anything. I just knew it was there.

Cath, from Glastonbury, England, was surprised by the psychic and spiritual awareness of her young son right from babyhood. When he was a baby, Dominic would never cry; instead, Cath would have a sudden urge to go to him. Dominic would be awake, quite motionless, but his eyes seeking her. She was never afraid of this power, and as Dominic began to talk, she always took what he said very seriously. On one occasion, he told her, 'I can see pictures in your mind.' On another occasion, when Dominic was quite little, his foreknowledge prevented what might have been a nasty accident. He told Cath to slow right down and almost immediately a car pulled out in front of her.

I have come across a number of similar cases in which an apparently inattentive young child will call out at a blind bend for the mother to stop the car. Invariably there is some unpredictable hazard around the bend and the child's words avert an accident.

As children get older and travel independently of parents, they can transfer this protective radar to themselves if they trust their intuitions and do not become too influenced by peer pressure. Kate, who lives in Wiltshire, England, was about 13 and a CB radio fanatic:

> I was going to an event, and some friends were giving me a lift to Trowbridge. Suddenly I had the most dreadful premonition that if I stayed in the car there would be an accident or something dreadful would happen to me, so I said, 'Can you drop me off, and I'll give you a call on the CB in half an hour?'
>
> They did, though they must have thought I was behaving oddly. Half an hour later, I tried to get through on the radio, but there was nothing on their waveband. About three-quarters of an hour later, I made contact with the boys' mum and discovered that the car had overturned and a tree had toppled over and gone through the back seat. The boys were all right, but had I been in the back seat I would have been killed.

Lesley's friend was not so fortunate. Lesley, who lives in Berkshire, England, told me how she and some friends had just got off the school bus one morning and were waiting at the kerb to cross over to school. 200 yards [185 metres] down the road, a car turned out of a junction into the main road leading towards the school. Lesley turned to her friend, Sylvie, and said: 'I think that woman is going to run you over.'

'She was shaking and there was something strange about her,' Lesley told me.

The woman stopped the car and some of the children crossed over. Sylvie stepped off the kerb, and Lesley tried to stop her, but she carried on going. The woman started up the car and ran Sylvie over. Luckily, Sylvie was only badly shaken and bruised.

A child can be spooked by such psychic experiences, especially if they have kept them to themselves. However, Lesley spoke to her mother, who was very open to psychism and was reassuring. But this didn't stop Lesley from being teased at school, where she was nicknamed 'Witchey-poo'.

### Joyful family premonitions

Though we most often hear about premonitions of disaster, some predictions made by children are happy ones, offering reassurance or announcing joyous events.

Maura, who lives in Mexico City, told me this experience, which happened some years ago:

> My second son, Omar, who is eight years old, has a special power to know the future. When he says this kind of thing, even though he is little, he becomes very serious, with a different tone in his voice, a tone that a child doesn't usually use.
>
> I had lost two babies, which had left me in a terrible depression. I was in bed, and Omar, then four years old, came by and stood by my side talking and playing. Suddenly he said very seriously and with that special tone in his voice, 'When my brother is 12 years old and I am seven years old, you will get pregnant again and this time we will have a baby.'
>
> Before this time I lost another baby (three babies in a row) and also lost all hope of having another child. My husband and I decided that we would not try again. Nevertheless, in January 1990, when my son Rodrigo was 12 and Omar was seven, I got pregnant again. This time my baby was born. He is four months old now. During this pregnancy I started to bleed as in the previous ones, so I told my sons not to get excited about the baby and to be prepared not to have him.
>
> Omar looked me straight in the eye and said, loud, clear and sure: 'This baby will be born.' Indeed it happened, as he foretold.

Psychic wartime links between family members are well documented, and children are especially tuned into absent members of the family. On page 22, I described how Fiona linked into the moment of her father's death at Dunkirk. In contrast, Jackie, who lives in San Diego, USA, predicted her brother's safe homecoming.

> When I was a teenager, my brother, Woodie, was in service in Japan. He had written to say that he was being processed to leave the service and so might not be in touch for some time.
>
> Exactly two months later, my stomach became upset due to a jittery feeling I had. I couldn't eat supper and wasn't sure why at first. Then it dawned on me that Woodie would be home tonight or tomorrow. I told my parents and they became a little angry with me and told me to stop such nonsense.
>
> The next day was worse. I sat on the sofa while my parents ate and wasn't even able to read the newspaper. There was a knock on the door. I jumped up and cried, 'It's Woodie!' I opened the door and there he was. My parents told me to 'stop that nonsense' but came running into the room when they heard his voice.
>
> Woodie had arrived in Ohio very late the previous night and decided to stay there overnight and make the rest of the 45-mile [117-kilometre] trip on the electric railway the next day. Otherwise he would have had to get us out of bed to come and get him from the station as there were no buses.

I have also come across cases of young children who know that their mother is pregnant even before she knows herself. This ability may reside in the strong bond between a young child and their mother but is nevertheless quite remarkable. Lin, who lives in Essex, England, described how her son Steven knew she was pregnant before she did.

> When Steven was four years old, he and his big sister Lucy were having a rough and tumble with me on the bed. Lucy was jumping all over me, and it was getting quite boisterous when Steven said to her, quite out of the blue, 'Be careful, Mummy's got a baby in her tummy.'
>
> His words shook me, as my husband and I had been trying for a baby for only two weeks and it had been a complete and utter secret. I told my husband and Mum and Dad, and we had a good laugh at what he had said.
>
> Two weeks later I discovered that Steven's uncanny prediction had come true: I was expecting another baby.

## Dream predictions

A number of children's predictions come in the form of dreams. Because the conscious mind is relaxed in sleep, the unconscious mind, which picks up information that the conscious mind blocks out, becomes more active. We dream five times a night – about every 90 minutes. We only remember a dream if we wake up during it. Even if we wake two minutes later, we have no recall of it, so the reported dream premonitions may be only a small number of the total examples of night-time psychic awareness.

When a young teenager dreams of a disaster, it can be very upsetting for them, because they are unable to prevent the disaster and yet they feel responsible. My own 16-year-old son, Bill, had vivid dreams of a major rail catastrophe for four or five nights before the Madrid train bombings in March 2004. He could not identify the station, but it was not in this country. He felt it should be Oxford, his local station, but it was not. Bill knew there was a bomb either by the train or on it, and when the train got to a station, it would blow up. He tried to warn people and stop the disaster, but he could not get anyone to listen.

Of course, there was a great deal in the news at the time about terrorists, but the timing was spot-on. After the incident, the dreams stopped. Because the dream was non-specific, Bill was frustrated that he could do nothing. He became very upset on the nights that the dream occurred prior to the disaster. I tried to reassure him, but he felt we should do something.

James's mother did not take him seriously when, at the age of 13, he told her he had dreamt about a huge boat sinking. James, from Oxfordshire, England, told me:

I had a dream about a big boat that left the harbour then went halfway out and crashed and was lying on its side. In the morning, I told my mum, and she said, 'Don't worry. You dream about all kinds of things.'

I was really worried and wondered if I ought to phone the police, but I was afraid they would think it was a stunt or I was a crank. Then two days later, on 6 March 1987, there was the Zeebrugge disaster, when the ferry, the 'Herald of Free Enterprise', tipped on its side as it left the harbour in Belgium.

Dreams about tragedies are common, and there are some well documented cases involving children. In April 1912, a 14-year-old girl in Nottingham told her grandmother about a dream in which a large boat kept sinking in the local park. The next day, news broke of the sinking of the *Titanic*. The girl's uncle, the ship's engineer, was among the dead.

After the Aberfan disaster in 1966, when part of a giant coal tip slid down on to a village school in South Wales, killing 128 children and 16 adults, Dr J C Barker made a nationwide appeal for premonitions about the tragedy. One account came from the parents of a ten-year-old victim. Shortly before the disaster, she had told her mother that she had dreamed she had gone to school and there was no school there. Something black had come down all over it.

All these dreams were different from ordinary nightmares because they were much more vivid and intense. In a premonitory dream, the dreamer may feel that he or she is living the dream, and the feelings may remain with them for several days.

But not all such dreams are about tragedies. Sheila, who lives in Southampton, England, described what seem to be her mind jumping ahead.

When I was 13 years old, one Friday night I dreamed that my mother asked me to get some meat from the butcher's, about 200 yards [185 metres] up the road. This was not unusual, as I regularly did errands on Saturday mornings. In the dream, the pavement narrowed as I approached a street lamp, and I had to step into the road around the lamp post, as a man and young boy were coming towards me. It seemed a typical meaningless dream until the next morning when my mother asked me to go to the butcher's.

As I reached the narrow part of the pavement where the lamp was, coming towards me were the man and the little boy who had appeared in my dream. As in the dream, I had to step into the road, around the lamp post. I had never seen them before in real life.

I was so spooked that I ran back home without getting to the butcher's. I still have a vivid memory of this. I am 71 years old now.

## Remote viewing

Remote viewing is when a viewer can detect an unknown object, person or scene in another place beyond the range of the physical eye, whether this is another room, another building or hundreds of miles away.

In Angela's case she was able to link into the picture of a person who was stealing from her home. From quite a young age Angela had found that she could control her dreams and use them to find out things that were going to happen in the future or to answer questions. When she was 14 and living in Alabama, the family were repeatedly having small items stolen from the home and suspected someone had a key. Before sleep, Angela asked who was coming into their house. She saw in her dream a young man taking a record player – his arm was coming through the window to steal it. Angela recognised him as the elder brother of a friend, whom she had seen once or twice. When the item she had seen in the dream was stolen while the family was away overnight, Angela was able to tell the police who the thief was. They found the stolen goods in his home.

## Coping with premonitions

For young children, a premonition may be forgotten by the time it comes true, and it is left to the parents to verify the original prediction. When my youngest son, Bill, was two years old, we were in the bedroom of our Reading home when Bill trotted to the window and said with interest, 'Fire in the sky.' It was quite a low window, and he was pointing over the house-tops. But I could see nothing. Next day he called me up to the bedroom again to see 'the fire in the sky'. This continued for about a week, with Bill pointing excitedly and me seeing nothing. Then a bakery caught fire about a mile and a half distant and the sky was filled with smoke and flames in the area Bill had shown me. I rushed upstairs to show him his fire in the sky, but he wasn't especially interested as he was playing with some new Lego. He had completely forgotten his words.

Older children and teenagers can become very distressed if they predict something they cannot prevent.

Teresa, from Surrey, England, issued a warning but was silenced. When she was eight, she was looking forward to going out in her aunt's car as usual on Saturday afternoon. It was always a treat, as they stopped somewhere nice for tea on the way back. But suddenly she had the most dreadful feeling that the car would crash. She told her mother, who was angry and told Teresa she was being silly. She said that if Teresa mentioned anything to her aunt, she'd get a smack.

Teresa couldn't forget her premonition. All the time they were out, Teresa was terrified, but she didn't dare say a word. When they finally pulled into Teresa's street, she heaved a sigh of relief, but at that moment a van pulled out of a side road and crashed into the side of her aunt's car. Teresa's mother insisted it was pure coincidence, and Teresa never told anyone about the incident till she was a mother herself.

Often the messenger gets the blame for bringing bad news, as Pat, from Reading, England, found out.

> I was 13, when one of my dreams came true for the first time. I woke up and did not want my breakfast. 'What's the matter with you?' Mum asked, in her usual brisk way. 'I had an awful dream someone was at the bottom of the pool,' I said, meaning the small lake in the town. Mum told me not to be stupid and sent me off to school.
>
> When I got home, the door was locked. It was never locked, so I was worried. I knocked, and Mum opened it. I will never forget her words. 'Your bloody dream!' she said. Her cousin, who had come for a visit, had drowned in the pool that day. Her sight was failing and she had mistaken the algae growing round the edge of the pool for grass and had walked on it. It was 40 years ago, but I can still remember how terrified I was and how furious my mother was. 'Your bloody dream!' she said.'

Even pleasant predictions can misfire. Dorothy, from Bracknell, England, now a grandmother, can remember going with her mother to a dancing club when she was 14. There she told a friend of her mother's: 'You are going to win the raffle.' The prediction was correct, but Dorothy found herself the target of a lot of anger, because everyone thought the raffle had been fixed.

Children whose psychic experiences are badly handled can feel isolated from others. Joy told me the story of her Aunt Florence, who was born in Nebraska in 1887.

> When Florence was about 13, she attended a sporting games day at her little school. They all sat in makeshift bleachers [raised stalls] to watch. Girls in those days were so prim and Victorian you couldn't believe it. Florence, being pretty, was especially afraid to call any attention to herself.
>
> In the middle of the game, Florence leaped up, shouted 'Run!' at the top of her little voice and dashed down to the field. When she looked up at everyone staring at her, she wanted to disappear in a hole. Immediately afterwards the bleachers collapsed. Many children were hurt.

Florence's gifts brought her little happiness. 'This aunt of mine was a much misunderstood woman and had a sad life,' says Joy.

Teenagers in particular may feel that they should have spoken out to avert a tragedy. Bernice, who lives in Wiltshire, England, told me:

> When my father was about 12, he was walking along a country road near his home. He saw three men building a tall wall and heard a voice say quite clearly, 'By tomorrow those three men will be dead.'
>
> Dad didn't know what to do. He was afraid to speak out in case the men were angry with him or he was wrong. But the next day he heard that the wall had collapsed and the three men had been killed. After that my father completely shut his mind to the psychic but found it hard to forgive himself for keeping silent.

In contrast, Alison, who lives in northern Scotland and who had had premonitions from the age of ten, spoke out about one of them.

> When I was a teenager, I told a man in a pub one night to be careful or he would turn his digger over. The next day my mother woke me to tell me that there had been an accident, and the man was in hospital after he tipped his digger over a wall and got trapped under it. Luckily, he was not seriously hurt.

Alison had in no way ill-wished the man, but had she not had a sensible mother and herself accepted her abilities, she might have felt illogically to blame.

## The power to change fate

While researching maternal instincts, I discovered a number of cases in which a mother foresaw disaster to her child. Though she could not alert them to the danger, she was able to pray, and so, it seems, prevent a potential fatality. This power seems to be limited to the child whom the mother feels protective towards, regardless of the age of the child.

The same power can be transmitted by a child to close friends and family, since children are more open than adults and seem to possess natural healing powers.

Jackie, who lives in San Diego, California, recalled:

> My landlady's ten-year-old daughter, Lucy, came to me and told me about a vivid dream that had frightened her. In the dream she had been badly injured in a car accident and her mother was crying over her. Lucy wanted to know if it would really happen. I told her I thought that if she prayed, perhaps she could prevent it.
>
> A year later I took Lucy and her sister for a drive, as I occasionally did. Their parents didn't own a car. But as I travelled along the four-lane freeway, I suddenly saw that ahead in the third lane, right on a curve, someone had abandoned a car with neither flares nor direction signals.

It was too late to swerve, because the other lanes were full, so I braked as hard as I could. I slid and hit the back end on the driver's side so hard it bent the front seat into a V, and I could hardly get out. But I only had a skinned elbow. Lucy had a skinned knee, and her sister a sprained thumb. They were in the back seat. A third car ran into mine and had a crashed fender.

The crash stopped traffic in all four lanes as far as you could see. No one who saw the wreckage could believe we had walked away alive. I think Lucy's prayer was most definitely answered.

Sally, who lives in Berkshire, England, told me she believes that the feeling of impending disaster that she and her mother shared prompted them to pray at the crucial moment when her brother was involved in a potentially fatal crash. Sally is convinced that because of this her brother's life was spared.

When I was 13, my mum worked shifts at the local hospital. One morning I woke up with the terrible feeling she was going to die. I didn't want to upset my mother by telling her, but I insisted I went to work with her. As the day progressed, I felt increasingly anxious. Mum, too, had a growing sensation that something dreadful was going to happen. She did not say anything to me, as she did not want to upset me. However, she did tell two friends at work about her fear. On the way home in the car, Mum suddenly said, 'Shall we stop at a church and say a prayer?'

I agreed and was incredibly relieved. Unknown to us, while we were praying, my older brother Anthony was involved in a car accident. Soon after we got home, there was a knock at the door. Mum said, 'Oh God! Something has happened to Anthony!'

It was a friend of Anthony's who had called to break the news that the car in which Anthony had been travelling was going too fast round a bend on a country road and had hit a tree. The police said all the occupants of the car should have been killed. Amazingly, Anthony and his friends walked away unhurt. I am convinced that we picked up the danger, although we did not understand it, and so were led to pray at the time when Anthony needed help most.

### When a younger child has a premonition

A true premonition is different from a fear experienced in a nightmare or a free-floating anxiety about a situation. A child will often speak about a premonition a number of times and refer to the event seen in the prediction as though it has happened or is happening. The details will not change in retelling, even over a period of days. Premonitions are rarely a narrative and may have vital details missing. The child will not attempt to fill these in but will look to you to explain and understand.

A very young child may have forgotten the premonition when the event does occur and may not express any sense of recognition.

Children who make regular predictions may become still and use a quieter tone of voice when they do so. Note down any obvious predictions and see how many come true, but do not make a big fuss about it. Talk about your child's premonitory abilities only to those you know will be sympathetic.

Whether or not you believe the child, take their words seriously and, if possible, reassure them that you will warn the person concerned (younger children's premonitions in particular are usually family-related). If the premonition concerns a place you go together, agree that you will not go at a time when they have foreseen a disaster occurring, but don't make a big deal about it. Similarly, if it is possible, follow the child's warning to slow down in the car or to slightly alter a travel plan. Obviously, it may not be practical to stop using the car entirely in response to a vague warning, but do check tyres, etc. regularly, and if you have been taking chances, show the child how you are now being more careful. If appropriate, you can also offer to say a prayer with the child or buy them a St Christopher medallion to protect them. At the worst, you will look a fool; at best, you will avert a potential disaster – though you may never be able to prove it. If the child turns out to be right, thank them.

If your child is always foretelling doom and gloom, they may be worried about safety generally. Cut down on the amount of news reports and scary programmes (sometimes broadcast even early in the evening) that they watch, and use their predictions as a chance to talk with them about their fears.

Ensure that bedtimes are calm and unhurried and that your child can unload the worries of the day. You could light a scented candle in a safe place in the bedroom and allow your child to blow it out before sleep, letting the light take away any fears and bad things from the day and transform them into starlight. (Never leave a candle burning in your child's room when you are not present.)

If a child talks about a parent dying, don't become alarmed or angry. This may simply be a separation anxiety, perhaps a result of them hearing about someone else's parent who has died. If there is marital tension, one parent is absent or one or both work away frequently, the child may also have unspoken fears of abandonment, which can manifest as premonitions that a parent will die. Such predictions are a good opportunity to offer the child reassurance about the parents' continuing relationship with the child and also to talk about any fears of mortality the child may have.

Don't feel spooked if your child can tell the future. As have I said, time is relative, and children do have greater access to their right-brain powers than adults.

## When an older child or teenager has a premonition

If your child has a premonition, accept what they are saying and do not try to minimise their feelings even for the best motives. Explain to the child that there are lots of ways in which we receive information and that some children and teenagers seem to be able to know things before they happen. This is quite normal, and the ability often lessens naturally as they get older.

Children and teenagers sometimes feel that they are responsible for causing a disaster that they have foreseen. Although this may seem illogical to an adult, the feeling is very real for the child. Explain that they are seeing something as though on a television screen and that they are in no way responsible for causing the disaster by foretelling it. If they feel that they should be able to prevent a wide-scale disaster, point out that in practice there is no way of doing this, because no one would listen, especially when the details of time and place are not clear. Never promise to phone someone official, even if your child is upset, because when they find out you have not made contact, they will lose trust in you.

Try to spend extra time with your teenager doing family activities, and if possible reduce their consumption of junk food, as artificial stimulants appear to increase anxiety and so premonitions that are free-floating rather than genuine.

If your older child or teenager warns you about family health or safety, see if you can tactfully warn the subject of the premonition without worrying or frightening them. The teenager may have picked up subconsciously that all is not well or the person is taking too many chances, perhaps, for example, by driving long distances without proper sleep.

If repeated premonitions are upsetting your child, teach them simple visualisation techniques to shut down their over-active psychic energies. For example, immediately after they wake from a nasty dream or have a feeling of doom, tell them to picture a sky full of stars and the stars going out one by one, leaving only velvety blue. Alternatively, give them amethyst crystals to put by the bed, as these seem to absorb fear. Suggest that they hold an amethyst in the centre of their brow for a minute or so. This is regarded as the site of the psychic, or third, eye. Amethysts will slow down the visions. Wash the stone afterwards.

# CHAPTER 4

# Invisible Friends

At least half the adults I have interviewed can remember an invisible friend in childhood, and sometimes still recall them in great detail and with affection. Surprisingly, few say that the friend was imaginary. Sometimes mothers are reluctant to talk about a child's invisible friend, even if they had one themselves, because of fears that their child will be regarded as odd for talking to someone no one else can see. Yet the phenomenon is entirely normal. Of course, some of these unseen companions can be explained by imagination. Others are used by the child to explain broken objects at home or to ask for extra sweets for their companion. But in a remarkable number of cases I have encountered, the friend is not used at all for advantage. The child may appear to know things that their friend has told them, which were not known by the mother and so cannot be explained as telepathy.

I will leave you to make up your own mind about the accounts in this chapter. I have focused on invisible companions who are children or animals. In the next chapter I will deal with guardian spirits, often a deceased grandmother who visits the child over a regular period.

## Who are invisible friends?

Let's start with some examples. Jan, now a mother of three who lives in Berkshire, England, is a rational, professional woman, yet she remains convinced that her invisible friend, Jellot, actually existed. Jan was sitting in a huge black pram when she first remembers seeing Jellot. She says: 'Jellot was pushing the pram with my mother. My mother told me I used to point at the empty space at the end of the pram.'

Jan's mother was always very worried by Jellot and insisted that Jan's friend was imaginary. This is understandable, because in the 1950s, at the time when Jan was young, acknowledging such companions was widely believed to encourage future mental instability in the growing child. Even today, hearing voices can cause parental anxiety, although invisible friends do generally fade away in their own time, usually when the child goes to school. They are never a sign of mental illness.

Jan next remembers Jellot when she was two or slightly older, in 1950 or 1951.

There were two air raid shelters at the bottom of the garden. I used them as a playhouse. Jellot lived in the shelters. I used to have to walk her back there when she had come shopping. I can still visualise her clearly. She wore clothes that weren't like mine – old-fashioned – and her brown dress used to come below her knee. You could see it under her coat, which she always kept buttoned up, even at the table. She wore a double-breasted camel coat with a collar. It was a rich material. She had brown shoes with buttons. The coat was soft to touch.

Jan used to try to make her mum hold her hand out for Jellot when they went out and used to scream because she wouldn't. Jan says that Jellot's hand felt warm to her and could be held like anyone else's. Jellot always had one sock rolled down and had curly, blonde, fly-away hair. When Jan played with the other kids in the street, Jellot would come.

When it was Jellot's turn to skip, the kids used to turn the empty rope. They tolerated her and I was under the impression they must be able to see her because I could.

One day I was sitting with Mum in our small front room, listening to 'Listen With Mother' on the radio. I was about four. I remember Mum was knitting a pink cardigan. There was a knock at the door and I went to answer it. Mum told me off for wandering away. 'I thought you were listening to your programme,' she protested. She hadn't heard the knock. I turned the big handle. Jellot was standing there with a woman.

'Oh, hello, Jellot,' I said. 'Yes, I'll tell Mum ... Mum, why has Aunty Bea died? ... Yes, she has. Aunty Bea's sister came with Jellot to tell me so I wouldn't be worried if I found out and didn't know.'

Aunty Bea was the lady over the road. Her sister was dead. Jan says she has no idea how she knew this was the old lady's sister.

Mum told me not to be silly, but after 'Listen With Mother' my mother did go over the road. She saw the old lady's nextdoor neighbour and asked if she'd seen Aunty Bea. She hadn't, which was unusual.

The neighbour came over later in the afternoon to say that Aunty had died in the night. When my father came home, my mother told Dad that Aunty Bea had died and I must have heard it from someone.

Jellot began to fade out of Jan's life when she started school: 'I didn't have time to go down to the air raid shelters any more. Then when I was seven they took down part of the shelters and she didn't come any more.'

But if Jellot had faded, 30 years later another invisible friend entered Jan's life. Her son, Ian, had a companion who appeared to come from the

France of several centuries ago. Because her mother had been so discouraging about Jellot, Jan was determined that it should be different for Ian, and she came to regard the invisible Andrix as almost another child.

Andrix first appeared when Ian was no more than 14 or 15 months old. He used to sit on the floor playing and handing toys to someone who was not there. Jan points out that Ian was not a solitary child, since he had a brother, Robert, who was 14 months older and, later, a younger sister. Of the three children, only Ian had an invisible playmate.

When Ian was three, he tried to tell Jan what Andrix was wearing. They had a velvet settee, and Ian used to run his fingers down the pile and say: 'That feels like Andrix's coat; that looks like Andrix's coat.' Jan says he was referring to the different colours you get when you smooth the pile. Andrix wore short trousers to the knee, very thin socks and shiny shoes. Ian told his mother that Andrix was French.

'How can you understand French then?' asked Jan. 'When you go to the other side, everyone talks the language,' replied Ian, who was not more than four. Jan said a few French words to Ian to see if he understood them, but he didn't. The family first went to France when Ian was five, and Andrix told Ian that if he (Andrix) went to France now, people would not understand him.

One evening, Jan found Ian apparently talking to Andrix in his bedroom, saying: 'It's all right. She's downstairs. She can't hear you. No, she won't come up, honestly.' (When talking to Andrix, Ian would leave the gaps, as if Andrix was replying.) The next morning, Jan found all Ian's toy cars with their bonnets up. Ian explained: 'Andrix doesn't know what an engine is, so I have to show him. They didn't have engines in those days. There wasn't an engine on horses, but you have horse power, don't you?'

When Ian was three he suddenly came out with the words, uncommon for a child of his age, 'cart ruts'. Andrix had told him that he had once fallen into a cart track. Ian recounted that the roads were always muddy in Andrix's time and told Jan about putting sacking under the cart wheels to stop them sticking in the ruts. Andrix was crossing over the road when he tripped on the ruts. 'It was very deep, Mummy,' Ian said. 'The mud actually came up to his waist.'

I asked Jan if Ian ever saw *The Three Musketeers* or similar programmes on television when he was young. She said that, no, they didn't have television on much when he was that age, and anyway Ian grew up on a diet of Thomas the Tank Engine. They had not been to France when Andrix first appeared and she cannot remember them specially talking about it.

Once Ian started school, he began to go to sleep earlier. He said that Andrix got very angry and used to say, 'You don't want to be my friend any more.' Ian would reply, 'I do, but I'm tired and have to go to school in the morning.'

Andrix disappeared for three months and then suddenly one evening Ian started playing with him. Then he disappeared for a while, came back, and then came no more. Jan dates his final disappearance to the time they moved to their present house, when Ian was seven.

Ian was 13 when he talked to me about Andrix.

> Andrix spoke French and another language so that everyone could understand him. He was always my best friend. I could see him and feel him. Whatever happened in the day, if I was told off and if I was angry with Dad or in a bad mood, if I was sad and sent to bed, I could tell Andrix and he would put it all right by the morning. He had brown hair with a queer parting flicked over to the left side.

Jan sees invisible friends as entirely positive and says that Andrix gave the family serenity and tranquillity and was a calming presence, just as Jellot had been in her own family 30 years before.

## Theories about invisible friends

There are many psychological explanations for invisible friends. The child psychologist Jean Piaget, whose theories revolutionised education, believed that a child's imagination stemmed only from what they had lived through and that the child grew out of fantasy as they became intellectually adapted to the real world. However, Piaget admitted the value of imaginary companions. His daughter, Jacqueline, had, among other friends, a strange bird-like creature that helped her in all she learned, gave her encouragement and consoled her when she was sad. However, none of this explains invisible friends from the past such as Ian's Andrix, which, if they were imagined, would necessitate the child knowing details of an earlier age that their intellect would not have been capable of absorbing.

Neither Jan nor her family are Spiritualists, but their feelings about Jellot and Andrix parallel the Spiritualist belief that invisible friends may be young children who were raised in the spirit world by loving relatives because they died young. They choose to come back sometimes to play with earthly children with whom they have some affinity. Because we naturally hate the idea of young children dying, this idea can seem very spooky to parents, but these presences are always benign. The children seem to stay with a specific child as long as they are welcome, before moving on to another earthly companion. I have occasionally come across cases where an adult will be shocked to meet a family, perhaps on the other side of the country, whose child has the same invisible friend, usually with a distinctive name or feature, as their own had when they were young.

Others believe that invisible friends are small angels who never lived before but are not yet strong enough to become full-blown guardian angels.

They appear in human or sometimes animal form so as not to frighten the child. With the belief in angels growing outside formal religious communities, more parents are now happy with this idea than when I wrote the first edition of this book.

## Invisible friends who seem more than imagination

In Chapter 2 I described Reice's experience with his great-grandfather. Angela also sent me an account of Reice's invisible friend:

> My four-year-old son has always spoken about what I thought was an imaginary friend. However, recently he has made me think that his friend may not be so imaginary. My son calls the friend Beeba. I asked why Beeba was his friend, and Reice said: 'There was a fire and Beeba was stuck. He tried to break the windows but couldn't and now Beeba's my friend.' The roof was made of straw. It was thatch.
>
> I was quite surprised at what he was saying, so I asked how old Beeba was. 'He's 19,' Reice told me, and he then drew a 1 and 9 in the air. At this time he was only just three and could only count to ten. At four years old he still can't write numbers, so I don't know how he managed to do it on that occasion.

When the British medium Doris Collins was a child, she had an invisible friend who turned out to be more than imagination. In Doris's case, her spirit friend opened the path to her future work as a medium. Doris was eight years old and staying with her aunt while her parents went abroad. The house had a huge garden. One day, while Doris was playing at the bottom of it, she saw a young girl coming towards her. The girl said she was called Connie and went to the school across the road. Doris and Connie played together every day.

One morning, however, it was raining, and Doris complained that she could not go out and play with her new friend, Connie. Her aunt asked Doris to repeat the name of her friend. Doris did and also described her new friend, telling her aunt that the little girl said she went to the school across the road.

Doris's aunt was very upset and told Doris that Connie had been her own little girl who died 12 years earlier. To Doris, as to other children who have encountered such friends, Connie was entirely real, solid and three-dimensional, and the girls held hands as they skipped. Connie's hands were warm. But Doris was never allowed to go outside and play in the garden again.

Joan, who lives in Southampton, England, had a similar experience to Doris's aunt but handled it very positively, with the result that her son's friend stopped coming naturally when he was no longer needed.

When my son Nigel was three years old, he had an imaginary friend he used to play with. We used to have to include him in everything and set a place at the table. When we went out, we had to take him with us. One day I asked my son what his friend's name was. He said 'Terry'. No way could he have known that before he was born we lost a baby at five months old. His name was Terry. Nigel stopped seeing his friend before he went to school, but at 56 he still remembers him.

David, who lives in Dudley, England, also believes that his friend was a brother who had died.

When I was four to six, we lived in Dudley town centre. Dad was a barber, and the shop was an old blacksmith's made into ladies' and gentlemen's salons. At the back were a living room, kitchen and back yard. The toilet was outside.

At about four or five years old, I had an invisible friend called Billy Bacon. I did not see Billy but I sensed him there. I did see his bike, and 54 years later I can still remember it. The bike had a dirty black frame and was about ten years old.

Billy and I did all sorts of things. What I did not know was that two or three years before I was born, Mum had lost her first child.

## When others see the friend

I mentioned on page 67 that sometimes more than one child can have the same friend. In Andrew's case, he and his sister, though born years apart, unknowingly shared the same invisible friend.

Andrew is now a 50-year-old publicity executive and lives in Somerset, England. As a child, he had an invisible friend called Haimayne, who looked like a lion with wings and a dragon tail. But Andrew never thought of Haimayne as invisible, for he left footprints in the snow and would move out of the way so other people would not tread on him.

Once, Haimayne saved Andrew's life. When Andrew was about eight, he climbed a steep cliff in the Mendip Hills and fell from the top. Some rock climbers from Guildford saw him fall about 30 or 40 feet (9–12 metres) and rushed to the bottom expecting to find him dead. However, Andrew picked himself up and limped off, helped home, he says, by Haimayne. Years later, he met one of the climbers, who commented on how Andrew had seemed to bounce five or six times as he fell, as if being caught on the way down, though this was impossible down a sheer cliff face. Andrew told me that Haimayne had run down beside him as he fell, trying to catch him.

One of Haimayne's earliest visits was when Andrew had been sent a long way on an errand and it got dark. Unexpectedly, it started to snow, and Andrew was lost in the middle of the countryside. He followed Haimayne's footprints in the snow all the way home. It was not until Andrew was 13 that Haimayne finally said goodbye to him, at the spot where they had first met. He came no more.

When Andrew was 21, his mother remarried and had a daughter, Becky. One day, when Becky was about three years old, Andrew went to visit. Becky told him about a friend who was like a winged lion the size of an Alsatian, with a dragon tail. She called him a cat dog with wings. She has a speech impediment, but she said the name was Heywain.

As an adult, Becky told Andrew that the name was actually Haimayne but she had been unable to pronounce it, and that he was yellowy-brown.

When Andrew was in Egypt, he saw some figures of Babylonian sphinxes – which have lion heads rather than the human ones on Egyptian sphinxes – and recognised his friend. I have continued this story in Chapter 10 (see page 175).

Just as intriguing is when another family member actually sees the invisible friend. Emma, who lives on the Isle of Wight, England, described her son's experience. Louis was two-and-a-half when he first mentioned Jack Grace to his mother, three years ago. Emma accepted her son's unseen companion.

> We used to hear Louis talking to someone in his room. At first it sounded as if he as talking to himself. We then thought, 'Hey, he is answering questions, so he must be talking to somebody.' The answers were just, 'Yes, yes,' and we would hear him laugh.
>
> I sat with Louis one day and asked what his friend looked like. Louis said he had yellow curly hair; he also had spikes down his back. I asked if this hurt, and he said yes and never mentioned that again. I asked what Jack liked to eat, and Louis told me lettuce. He also said that he smelt, lived in a local town – Shanklin – had never had a mum and dad and that his name was Jack Grace. I asked one day where Jack Grace was now. Louis said, 'He's gone now. He's in heaven.'
>
> Louis did not speak of him again. A few months later, I again asked Louis, 'Where is Jack Grace?' Once again Louis said, 'I've told you. He has gone.'
>
> Louis had visits from Jack Grace for about two years. Then it just stopped.
>
> About a year-and-a-half ago I was in my bedroom and it was very late. I was aware there was someone in my room. At the bottom of the bed was a little boy, about eight years old, with curly hair. In my mind I asked, 'Why are you here?' He replied, 'To see Louis.' I was not frightened, just mesmerised by the whole thing. Then he was gone. I was left stunned and overwhelmed. I was also feeling very hot for some reason and cried and cried. Eight years previously I had miscarried at five months. Was Jack Grace telling me that the children we have lost are always with us?

## Dealing sympathetically with invisible friends

Usually, where a parent or a grandparent allows a child to talk freely about an invisible friend – as any other good friend – the event does not take on undue importance. As suggested by the cases above, when the child goes to school they generally become too busy with earthly friends or too tired to maintain the unseen friendship.

When Luke, who lives in Reading, England, was four-and-a-half, he became obsessed with an invisible friend called Derek. Pat, Luke's grandmother, told me that Luke chatted almost non-stop to him about everything under the sun. However, Liz, Luke's mum, became very frightened, so Luke talked mainly to his grandma about Derek. Pat told me:

> I asked Luke if I could talk to Derek, but Luke replied, 'Derek says he doesn't like grannies.' Luke told me that Derek had been badly burned during the War, and I wondered whether Derek could be the spirit of a wartime child, as Luke's house was an old one and I had often sensed strange things there. Then Derek disappeared, and Luke didn't talk to him or about him any more.
>
> I understood, because when I was no more than three or four years old myself, I had a very special invisible friend called Barbara Jean. Unlike Luke, who is one of four, I was very lonely as a child, and Barbara Jean was my dearest friend. I can still recall Barbara Jean going up the alleyway to school with me. It was overhung with trees and very dark, especially in winter, and I was terrified of witches. Barbara Jean stayed with me till I was about six, though I didn't dare to talk to Mum about her, as she told me such things were all nonsense and got very cross with me when I mentioned my friend.

Angie wasn't allowed to talk of her invisible friend at home, but her sister was.

> My sister's invisible friend was a boy called Arby. The friendship lasted for several years, until she eventually made friends with a real little boy called Harvey when she was about seven. My sister's friend was out in the open, and my mum knew all about him and allowed him to sit at the table and go places with us, but my invisible friend had to be secret. Mine didn't even have a name. Maybe that's why I don't even know if it was a boy or girl. I wasn't lonely, as I had a big sister and lots of friends.
>
> But my invisible friend was special and always with me, though I was very careful never to answer him if he spoke when anyone else was around, which sometimes happened. I wondered later if my friend was the little girl next door, who had been killed in a car accident just before we moved in. It was strange and very hurtful having to hide my friend when Arby was so welcome, but Mum got very annoyed if I so much as mentioned my friend and told me not to be a baby.

Cheryl, who lives in Newport, Isle of Wight, England, was allowed to make her invisible friend part of her everyday life and so recalls the experience with great happiness, though the details have faded.

> When I was three, I had an invisible friend. I cannot recall much about him, but my mother can. He went everywhere with me. It got to the point where, when my mother travelled on a bus with me, I had to sit on her knee so my invisible friend could have a seat. When I had sweets or chips, my mother would have to buy an extra lot, but strangely enough I would never eat them, so it wasn't just an excuse. Then, when I was about four, my invisible friend stopped.
>
> Dad built me a wooden slide and I insisted that someone called Cock-a-doodle-doo lived under it and I had to protect him from everyone. My uncle still jokes about him.

## Animal companions

Andrew and Becky's invisible friend was a dragon. A number of children have animal companions. David, who lives in Shrewsbury, England, wrote to me about his magic birds:

> I was born in Burma in 1948. My father was a missionary clergyman. I have no conscious memories of Burma but remember my grandmother's large house in Fordingbridge in Hampshire, where we stayed for a few months after returning home pending my father's appointment to the incumbency of St Gluvias, Penryn, in Cornwall.
>
> St Gluvias had a typical large vicarage with about two-and-a-half acres [just over an hectare] of wildly uncontrolled garden. Perhaps an acre of this was wooded copse with mature oak, ash, lime and other full-sized trees, and dense bushes, brambles and dense undergrowth. My sister was about three years younger.
>
> I had as my bedroom a large first-floor room with a bay window looking directly towards 'the jungle'. As I lay in bed in the darkness, I remember seeing the dark outlines of the trees through the uncurtained window. In the trees I saw something that I called coloured birds. They were luminous creatures about the size of birds that moved occasionally through the branches. When they moved, they left a trail of light that soon faded. There were many of these birds within the field of view framed by the window, and always one or two on the move.
>
> I remember the vivid colours and the curious depth and beauty of the creatures, and the wonder and excitement I felt at the time. I never got out of bed to look more closely. I remember saying to myself, 'I'll look in the morning', and promptly falling asleep.
>
> I never thought of these creatures as angels, in spite of my devout environment. I cannot remember telling my mother then,

but years later I described them. My mother said I was probably dreaming of the parrots in the jungle. This I accepted, but then I read a description of psychic globules of light playing around and on trees and plants during the hours of darkness, and I now wonder if my child's mind caught a glimpse of this.

Jean, who comes from Doncaster, England, told me some years ago of how her daughter had not only unseen animal friends but also a farmer to care for them:

My seven-year-old daughter, Ellen, has a invisible friend she calls Farmer Fields. Recently, her teacher gave the class a spelling test then realised she'd given the children the wrong test, one that was intended for the class a couple of years above. To her surprise, my daughter, who is no great speller, was the only child to get all the answers right. Ellen didn't tell her teacher the reason but explained to me: 'It was easy. Farmer Fields whispered all the answers to me.'

Farmer Fields, according to Ellen, runs an invisible farm that doesn't have ordinary animals but gryphons and unicorns. One morning we were going to school when she stopped by a field and started to cry. 'The fire is burning the field and my unicorns are sick. They are going into their realm,' she told me.

The next day on the way from school we saw that the real farmer was burning the stubble in the field and it was all scorched.

## Invisible foes

Very rarely, an invisible character may be frightening to the child. Often this coincides with a stressful period in the child's life. In this case it is important that the child is given strategies and support to defeat the invisible foe and that the fears are taken seriously. I have written more of this in Chapter 6.

Edmund, now 26, lives in Plymouth, England. He was haunted by a creature he called 'the lion with glasses' for a period of 18 months, from when he was about two-and-a-half until he was four. This was a traumatic period for Edmund, during which his separated parents were reconciled and moved to a new home.

I remember the lion with glasses very well. He was in my bedroom in the big white house. I used to be sent to my bedroom while my father was having his lunch, because he did not like me around making a noise.

I saw the face on top of the curtains, hanging out looking over me, the lion with glasses. He was yellowy-brown. He stared at me. I was very scared of him. He looked horribly at me as if he was going to kill me and jump out at me. I used to hide behind my wardrobe until someone came upstairs. He changed shape when people came so he wouldn't look so fierce. I knew he was real when I was small.

I think now it was just the shape of the curtains. When the wind blew, he looked bigger. He was only in that house, in that bedroom. I used to dream about him. He was really awful, horrible, in my dream. He used to peer in at my curtains. I used to try to get out of bed, but a force held me. He said, 'You're going to die. I hate you for living in this house.' I couldn't move. Now, when I remember that, I think perhaps he was real. The force was holding me. The lion was talking: 'Nobody enters my dream.' He had a horrible voice. He looked over me with his great glasses. He was just a head. Every night I had dreams about him.

When we moved away, it was completely different. It was after Christmas that he came. After we went out in the road and I got a sweet from Father Christmas on his sleigh. Then the lion said, 'I hate you for living here. It's my house.'

It was not the same room in my dreams. The windows were open and the door was locked. The lion was velvety. I liked the skin of the lion. He had big round glasses, the same colour as my dad's. He was a very realistic lion. Sometimes when the wind was blowing, his face was twisted up. Last time I saw him, he said, 'I'm going.' He was not there the last couple of nights before we moved.

Edmund's mother said:

I can remember the lion almost as well as Edmund. He came as soon as we moved to the south-west of England and a white house with big rooms, high ceilings and ornate curtain rails. It was not a happy house. It was meant to be a new start after a separation.

I was pregnant with my second child, but my then husband found the noise and mess of a toddler difficult to cope with. I was trying to be good wife and mother and found the two conflicted. Edmund was shut in his room while my husband ate lunch. Edmund found family meals traumatic, so it seemed less stressful to feed him first.

The lion was a real problem in our lives. It was not until I left my husband that the lion went, when Edmund, the baby and I moved away to an old cottage in a market town about 20 miles away. Edmund said the lion told him he was going off. I thought we were the ones to leave the lion. Perhaps we were both right.

Helen Manning, a child psychotherapist who helped the family commented:

It must have been a fearful time for Edmund. Change was in the air with the arrival of the baby. The parental relationship was rather uncertain. How does a child make sense of moving house, parental disharmony, new baby, etc.? In some way, maybe, this lion was the expression of the threat the child was experiencing.

Whether the lion was a psychic or a psychological manifestation, at the time it was terrifyingly real for Edmund.

Though an invisible foe may seem laughable to adults, it can hold a young child in sheer terror. Ben, who lives in Hampshire, England, was only three when an invisible cockerel that bit his toes terrified him. He had never had a bad experience with a cockerel in the everyday world. Ben's mother tried shooing it away and even offering it corn and birdseed, but Ben could still see the cockerel, and it continued to menace him. Indeed, when a child sees an invisible foe, it is no good anyone else saying that the it has gone unless the child himself accepts the departure scenario.

Ben was under stress because he was a very intelligent and unusually articulate child who was having great difficulty fitting into the local playgroup. His father was away most of the time with work, and the family had not long moved to a small village where newcomers were regarded with suspicion.

At last Ben's mother decided to ask Ben himself how they could get rid of the cockerel. 'Send him back to where he came from,' Ben replied, and Ben knew exactly where cockerel's home was. It was the farm park about five miles down the road, which Ben loved and where he would happily feed the poultry and other birds. Ben devised a plan to catch the cockerel in a large bag and throw him up into the sky so he would fly home.

After a couple of false starts, this was accomplished to cries of, 'Off you go, cockerel, and don't come back!' The cockerel came back several times, but Ben didn't mind because he had the power to banish his invisible foe.

Ben's mother was very understanding about what was a figment of her son's imagination. Or was it? A couple of weeks after cockerel's final departure, Ben and his mother went to the farm park. Ben rushed over to the enclosure where the hens and cockerels were and picked out a particularly malevolent-looking black cockerel. 'Hello, cockerel,' he said with a delighted smile. 'It's me, Ben.' And his mum says the creature left the others and came over to see them.

Fortunately, invisible foes are very rare. If the child is having a negative psychic experience as a result of earthly family problems (and this is not always the case), resolution may lie in dealing with the underlying conflicts. Often then the foe will disappear as if by magic, or at least be more readily overcome by the child.

### When a child has an invisible friend

Do not be spooked by a child's invisible friend or fear that your child is hearing voices. Invisible friends are, as you can see in this chapter, very common and quite normal. Most invisible friends fade away when the child starts school if they are not made into a big deal or a dark secret.

Go along with the child if they ask you to set an extra place at the table and so on, but do not let the presence of an invisible friend disrupt your routine or allow a child to get away with bad behaviour. Explain that invisible friends, like all family members, have to keep house rules and that your child is not allowed to eat an invisible friend's sweet ration or offer a seat to the invisible friend when an earthly family member needs it.

Make sure your child has plenty of human companionship with children their own age and that there are plenty of family activities.

If you suspect that the invisible friend is a little spirit child, do not be afraid. The innocence of children gives them inbuilt protection against harm. There is no way your child will be possessed (that only happens in very bad films that are entirely fictitious).

Document your child's experiences, as details may fade and they are part of the family heritage. If you had an invisible friend yourself, tell your child about them, as you would share any other childhood memory.

If a child is frightened by an invisible friend, do not laugh at the child or let anyone else tease them about what is a real fear. An unsympathetic approach will cause the child to keep other fears to themselves and thus feel isolated.

Do not worry that your child is odd, but focus on making the child feel more powerful and in control. Ask your child to help you to devise strategies you can carry out together to send the foe away and be prepared to repeat them until the child is happy.

Make sure there are no earthly tensions, such as bullying by a sibling or at school, or frequent arguments between parents. Encourage your child to talk about general fears and worries, and offer what reassurances you can without making false promises.

# CHAPTER 5

# Childhood Angels and Spiritual Guardians

Guardian angels and spiritual guardians, it would seem, also protect children. These spirit guardians are often older relatives who feel an affinity with the child, even if they died years before the child was born. Others are former residents of a house where the child lived and who love children.

Rarely does the child feel any fear, and they may draw great comfort from being cared for, if angels and spirit guardians manifest – as they often do – when the child is feeling alone or anxious. Angelic appearances are usually also acceptable to parents, though they may not always believe that the angel is real. Nevertheless, some parents are spooked by the idea of a deceased grandmother, grandfather or other benign adult guardian watching over their child. This is partly because the modern westernised world has made death into a taboo subject, with departed relatives firmly locked away in the ground or in heaven. In earlier times, the concept of protection from a wise ancestor was considered a blessing, and still is among societies whose ways have remained relatively unchanged into modern times.

## Angelic experiences

I met Myrtle when I attended Quaker meetings in Reading, England, with my children some years ago. She was in her eighties then, very wise and an inspiration to everyone. She told me this story from her own early life.

> When I was a child in southern India, several little angel friends used to come and play with me. In the afternoons I would be put for a rest on the verandah, and the angels used to stand on the balustrade and come down to play if I called to them. Sometimes they stood around my mattress and told me tales of how they helped people who were in trouble, guided them over difficult mountain passes and through hazardous places and protected them from danger. I never told anyone my secret. It was too precious.
>
> When I was 13, I was sent to England to boarding school. I was so far from home and I was very miserable. But my angel friends helped me and stayed with me until I settled down. I still think

about my angel friends, as they were such an important part of my early life, and sometimes now I feel their presence.

I recently learned that Myrtle had died.

Most children have only a single angelic experience. My son Jack saw an angel when he was six. He told me about its visit as we were walking down to the local beach. 'I saw an angel outside my bedroom window last night,' he said. 'I had a bad dream and when I woke up there she was.'

'What was she like?' I asked.

'You know,' Jack said, 'like an angel, wings and a white dress. Do you think it could be a clockwork angel?'

Jack was just leaving the magical stage and trying to explain things to himself. I said I didn't think so but asked him if he thought it was perhaps a fairy.

'Mum,' he said, as though talking to a two-year-old, 'angels are angels and fairies are fairies. Can we have some crisps?'

Annette, from Glasgow, Scotland, saw an angel but was very hurt when her parents didn't share her excitement.

> When I was ten, my parents and I went to stay in Glasgow. I was in bed, recovering from a bout of flu. It was about two in the afternoon when I looked up at the wall facing my bed and saw an angel. She was a lovely woman in a long, flowing gown, with long, flaxen hair. She appeared to come from the outside wall and floated across the room and disappeared out of the other wall.
>
> I jumped out of bed to tell my mother, and she said I must have been dreaming, but I know I was wide awake. I remember feeling very excited when I saw the angel and wanting my parents to know. My father was cleaning his shoes ready to go to work when I rushed in with the news. The experience made me feel very special for a long time, and I told my best friend I was 'the chosen one'. My grandma had just died and we had been very close.

Rosemary is a teacher. She was a mother in her thirties when she told me about the angel she had seen as a child. Again, her mother tried to explain away her experience.

> When I was about six, we were living in a rented house in Northern Ireland. It was a strange old house. I was ill in bed. The curtains were drawn, but the room looked out on to the back garden. I suddenly saw a beautiful golden angel with wings. It was the size of an adult. I wasn't frightened but just lay in bed looking at the wonderful angel. I felt it was the right time to see an angel, as there had been a lot of illness in our family.
>
> I told my mother, but she completely disregarded the experience. It was so disappointing. She insisted that it must have

been just a light shining on the side of the house. But it wasn't, as there was no light for miles, and I knew my angel was real.'

Mary, who lives in Mid-Wales, isn't sure whether her angel was dream or vision, but it remains, even in her adult life, a very special experience.

When I was 12 or 13, I had a dream in the middle of the night that there was a bright light shining outside my bedroom window. I got out of bed and felt my way downstairs to the room below mine to get a closer view. The curtains were not drawn because the room was rarely used. It looked out on to the garden and to the wall and the window of the convent next door. Framed by the window were three angels formed of golden light rays. I do not know how long the vision lasted, nor do I remember going back upstairs to bed. In the morning I felt as if it had not been a dream at all. I wasn't sleep-walking and am sure I left my bed that night.

Rhona, from Swansea, Wales, explained how her angel stopped her fearing the dark:

When I was 12, I saw an angel. I remember waking one night and looking at the top of my bed. There it was, about two feet [60 centimetres] high. It had a long white garment with a yoke, and a halo around its head. The hands were joined as though in prayer. Somehow I knew I must not speak to it or it would go away, so I went back to sleep. I was not so afraid of the dark after that and felt as though a great burden had lifted from me.

If a child is encouraged to talk about their experiences they may be open to more regular contact with these special guardians. Angela, who lives in Kansas, wrote to me after an article about psychic links appeared in the *National Enquirer*. She told me:

My eldest child, Julia, has had many experiences with angels who saved her from falls. She has seen a sparkling angelic being and has a great belief in God. Angels have also visited Eleanor, my second child. A ball of light came to her, and the rest of the family was scared. But Eleanor said, 'Don't worry, Mom. It was just an angel like you explained to me.' Eleanor sees balls of light often.

## Working with angels

Occasionally an early childhood experience can awaken an interest in spirituality that is developed in later years. Lita de Alberdi, who runs the School of Living Light in Somerset and is a respected angelologist, began her professional work as a result of her own early experiences with angels.

When I was a child, I saw angels around my bed, and I had a strong feeling that they were protecting me as I slept. When I was about eight, I saw an angel when I went to church with my school for the harvest thanksgiving service. I saw a wonderful shaft of light coming down from the high ceiling of the church, and a shining angel was part of this heavenly light. No one else had noticed it.

Jacky Newcomb, a journalist and angelologist who lives in the north of England, has recently published a book called *An Angel Treasury* (see page 186). She first sensed her guardian angel in childhood.

The Isle of Wight to the south of England was a favourite family holiday zone for my parents. The beautiful white sand was probably the thing I remember the most – well, that and a strange experience I had ...

Mum was sorting out the picnic and Dad was reading the paper. We were sitting within the shade of our windbreak, and my youngest sister (still a baby) was wiggling her toes in the hot sand. My middle sister and I were building sandcastles and trying to fill up our castle moat with water, walking endlessly to the sea to collect water in our buckets.

The picnic was ready, but I wanted to do just one more run back to the sea to fill up my bucket. The sand was scorching hot, so it crossed my mind that a dip in the water before the long walk back up the beach was a good idea. I couldn't swim, so I picked up my rubber float to carry down to the water's edge.

The water was beckoning me in the heat of the sun. Maybe I'd walk a little deeper into the sea – just for a moment. In seconds I was bobbing up and down in the sea. My family were way off in the distance, and the beach was now crowded with families and children. In no time at all I could feel myself being swept out to sea!

The breeze had picked up, and I was being pulled towards a nearby crop of rocks. I didn't understand a lot about death, but I knew at that moment that I was going to drown and there was nothing I could do about it. I was panicking like crazy and wondering what to do.

Moments later I realised I was not alone. I was surrounded by a peaceful presence, which seemed to communicate with me somewhere inside my head – a voice that was not a voice. I was enveloped by a serene calm and an inner contact that was separate from my own consciousness. It was something that wasn't me. The voice spoke to me inside my mind: 'You can drown if you want to ... or you can swim to shore,' the presence seemed to say.

'Swim to shore? But I can't swim.'

'The presence will help you. You can swim to shore.'

It made me feel in control. I realised that I could do this and I started to move my arms as I had before, but this time I felt stronger. I started to swim. I was beating the waves. Closer and closer I got the shore, stronger and stronger I felt, and all the time I was being moved forward by an unseen force and guardian, something or someone that wanted to help me ... was it my guardian angel?

It took me a long time to get back to the beach, and I wondered if I'd suddenly learnt to swim – I hadn't. I stupidly went back into the water and came up coughing and spluttering. Even more bizarrely, my swimming aid hadn't helped me to stay afloat at all. When I looked down, the air had completely gone! What had just happened? An inner voice, a presence, my angel had saved me from drowning.

I rushed back to the family. 'Where have you been?' asked my mother.

'I nearly drowned!' I cried breathlessly.

'Never mind, have a sandwich.'

And that was the end of that. I knew that something amazing had happened, but it was filed away until many years later. Now I work with the angel energy for a living. I teach angel workshops and write books and magazine articles about angels.

## Psychic or spiritual experiences?

Children do not recognise the same strict boundaries and categories that we impose in adulthood, in which one experience is classed as spiritual and another as psychic. I could equally have called this book *The Spiritual Powers of Children.* I believe that any experience in which a child uses their own innate gifts, whether to read their mother's mind or to see an angel or a deceased relative, is an expression of spirituality of the highest order.

Paul, from Dorset, England, told me about his two sons, who see both angels and their deceased grandmother, who acts as a guardian.

Our youngest son, Sam, who would have been five-and-a-half at the time, started saying that he was seeing my mother. She passed away in 1996, when he was only six months old. This was two years ago now, and he still says Granny comes to see him at night and plays games with him and cuddles him when he cannot sleep.

Our eldest son, Aaron, who is 11, saw an angel standing behind my wife Patricia, wrapping its wings around her. On another occasion, he saw a lady sitting beside her on the couch, with her arm linked with hers. Aaron also sees colours around people, especially teachers at school and friends.

Also, when he was going to sleep one night, he saw little white angels above his bed on a white cloud and had a feeling of someone sitting on his legs. Our youngest son came into the room and said to his brother: 'Granny is sitting on you.' We were just amazed.

Kayleigh, whose telepathic experiences with her grandmother I described on page 25, had an invisible friend who always appeared when her grandmother, Sylvia, was ill. Corrine, Kayleigh's mother, says:

All I know is the friend was a girl and had a foreign-sounding name. When my daughter spoke of her, I could never get the name right. But her great-grandma, who passed away before Christmas, has now taken over that role. Kayleigh speaks to her now, and the invisible friend seems to have gone.

My daughter recently told me that she went to visit her great-grandma in the sky and they had lots of fun throwing darts at a round board. Kayleigh said she could not quite reach, and a man she called Granddad lifted her up. My mum asked around and discovered that my grandma's first husband played darts. But I never knew him, and so Kayleigh certainly knew nothing about him.

## Guardian spirits

Children are also cared for by guardian spirits, sometimes also called spirit guides. These tend to be very good at helping with practical everyday concerns. Whereas an angel never lived on earth, most spirit guides were once wise humans and have chosen to guide others in the afterlife.

Pauline, who lives in Lancashire, England, heard her helpful guide as a voice in 1933, when she was 13, and she never forgot the experience.

Dad was out of work and things were desperate at home. He had a pair of worn-out boots, his only ones. He mended all the family's shoes expertly on an iron foot but just could not afford to buy a sixpenny piece of leather from the cobbler's.

I was on an urgent errand to the Co-op for three-pennyworth of bacon and was thinking about Dad as I hurried along. I was walking on some broken pavement. Weeds and dock leaves grew through the cracks. As I walked, a clear loud voice said in my ear, 'Look down among the dock leaves and you will find sixpence.'

I knelt down and felt inside and out the green clumps, but it was not there. Then I saw a clump growing almost out of the wall. I felt carefully around each leaf till at last I made contact with a silver sixpence. I fled with it to the Co-op and came home with a large bag of bacon pieces and a hock.

That put a smile on Mother's face. With plenty of potatoes and root vegetables, we were assured of dinner for the next two days.

Mum and Dad accepted the story that I found the sixpence. I was brought up to be honest, but I couldn't tell them about the voice. Dad got the leather to repair his boots and soon after was offered a job as a drayman to the corn merchant at the mill nearby.

Jennifer, who lives in Southampton, England, described how her son was led to his future profession by what seems to have been a spirit guide.

My son James was born on 19 May 1978. My father died 18 months later. Obviously, during the following months I would go to the cemetery to take flowers to my father's grave. On several occasions while my mother and I were tending the grave, James would be about 12 feet [4 metres] away, sitting on a gravestone chatting and laughing. James was a very early talker and was very fluent before he was two.

One day when we called him, he said he was talking to his friend. Going along with him, we asked about his friend. He said his name was Bernard. What an unusual name to dream up, I thought, since this was not a name any of us was familiar with.

The following week, the wire basket in which the dead flowers were placed was full, so we had to walk along the graves to the other path where there was another basket. We stopped. The name on James's friend's headstone was Bernard

On another occasion, James was dancing and laughing to himself on the grass that was yet to be used for a grave. When we called him, he said Bernard's friend was playing a pipe and he wanted James to dance. Every week, James would dance to the pipe and talk to Bernard. Only he could hear the pipe.

So adamant was James that he wanted to dance that he started dancing lessons at three years old. He was British under-21 ballroom dancing champion and has now turned professional at 26. I suppose we should really look up Bernard's details and find why he chose to talk to James.

James and I have a psychic bond. I will dial his number and get the engaged signal, as he is dialling mine. I will phone to ask him over to tea as he is phoning to see if there is any tea going.

## Offering a helping hand

Ruby, who lives in California, was helped by an invisible guardian when she was young and anxious. She told me that when she was seven years old and living in Nevada, her stepmother had to go into hospital suddenly for an operation. Her Aunt Carrie, whose house she had visited only once when she was very young, was picking Ruby up from the school playground to take her to her home on the other side of the city.

> My aunt was late, so I decided to find my own way. In a few minutes I was completely lost and terrified in an unfamiliar part of town. I prayed for help, and a voice told me to follow it and I would be shown the way. I wasn't worried any more and followed the directions I was being given. I arrived at my aunt's home to find a total panic. My aunt was there very upset, and search parties were out looking for me. No one could believe I could possibly have found my way, as I didn't even know the address.

Carole who lives in Reading, England, told me:

> When I was a small child, there were three holes in my bedroom curtain. Through the holes I could see a big blue eye. I knew there

was someone out there looking after me. The eye wasn't always there. Sometimes I could just see the moon.

My grandparents lived next door. I remember when I was six or seven I was sent next door with a message. It was teatime and winter, so though it was only about five o'clock, it was pitch-black. It seemed such a long way from their gate and through the dark entry to their back door. I stood at the back gate, frozen with fear, and can remember saying, 'I can't get there.'

Suddenly, I was lifted off the ground by someone I couldn't see, carried all the way to the back door and put down gently. I didn't tell anyone because I felt it was a very special thing. Afterwards I was much less scared, because I knew for sure I was being looked after.

When I was about eight, I fell out of a tree. I was with my cousins, Gill and Peter, in the garden of a pub by the River Thames. I had climbed the tree and was quite high up when I lost my grip and fell backwards horizontally. As I fell, I cried to my guardian angel, 'Please come and help me.'

Afterwards, my cousins said it was as if I fell in slow motion and landed not with a bang but as though there were cushions under me. I got up with hardly a scratch or bruise where I should have been really badly hurt. Again I knew I was being taken care of. But I made my cousins promise not to tell any of the adults, who were fortunately out of sight, as we'd have got into dreadful trouble for climbing the trees.

Nikki, whose experience of frightening ghosts in the mirror is described on page 46, told me how, when she was 17, she was driving a Citroen C4 towards her aunt's old house, where her aunt was holding a spiritualist meeting. She was in a hurry and was tearing along the lane, at the end of which was a main road with a stream of cars going along. There was no time to brake.

Time stopped and I did not hear a screech. The car floated slowly over another car whizzing along the main road. It landed with a bump on the other side and carried on. We were saved by an invisible presence.

### Grandparents who come back

For most children, however, it is a grandparent who lovingly watches over them, as they would have done during their lifetime. Children have an amazing knack of picking up the kind of irrelevant detail in their experiences with their deceased grandparents that confirms to adults that the experience was more than childish fantasy. It may be easier for young children to make contact because they don't have the same barriers of logic or disbelief. Gran is still Gran whether she has died or just popped round the corner to do the shopping.

Since her death, George's late wife, Celia, has made contact with several family members. But it is with her granddaughter, Jane, that the closest bonds have remained. George, who lives in Nuneaton, England, is entirely happy about this.

> My three-year-old granddaughter, Jane, can see my late wife. A few weeks ago she was out in my garden. We could hear her talking and saying, 'Nanny, Nanny,' and a whole lot of conversation in between. When she came in, she pointed to my wife's photo three times, saying quite spontaneously, 'That's Nanny in the garden.'
>
> When Jane got home, her mother remarked, 'I heard you talking to Nanny.'
>
> 'Oh, yes,' replied Jane. 'Nanny told me she wasn't wearing her usual dress today. Her new one is purple. That's God's colour.'
>
> The strange thing was, the same night my daughter-in-law, on holiday in Florida, dreamed she was in the garden with Celia but she could not see her. Then she saw a small purple waterfall and my wife was there, dressed in purple too.

This was not the first contact Jane had with her granny. George explained:

> I decided to have Celia buried in a pink dress and pink shoes, but of course my granddaughter did not see her and was not told about the choice of clothes. One Sunday, not long after, Jane started waving and smiling. Her mother asked who she was waving to, and Jane replied, 'Granny went by in the sky.'
>
> Her mother asked what Granny was wearing, and Jane said her pink dress and shoes. Jane often says she plays outside with Granny, and when she was told on one occasion to come in out of the rain, turned and said, 'Hurry up, Granny, or you will get wet too.'

Another Jane, who lives in Lincolnshire, England, wrote to me about an experience that happened when she was 16 years of age. It convinced her that her late grandmother was still with her.

> When my grandma died I was only eight years old, and she was like a second mother to me. Years later I got into some trouble with my mum, and I thought now my gran was dead I had no one to talk to.
>
> The problem I had with my mum was the usual teenage one of growing up, and we had an argument. It was a Sunday in October, and after the quarrel I went with my other grandma to the graveyard to visit my gran's and my grandmother's mother's grave. When we left the graveyard I felt very lonely.
>
> For the first time since Gran had died, I smelled her perfume very strongly and I heard her call my name. I turned round and saw my grandma standing there in the road, just smiling at me. I

felt warm and comforted by her and knew she was telling me that she was there and would never leave me.

I only told my mum some weeks after the event, but I don't think she believed me. It's not frightening to see a loved one. It's a nice experience of warmth, love and a sense of knowing what will happen after you die.

I do believe now that when I have a problem that I can tell no one else, she is still there. I can feel her and it makes me feel better knowing she is still there for me.

## Voices from the past

Children can also see relatives who died years before they were born and whose identity they may not know. This was the case with Lindsay whose experiences with her late brother Robbie I described on page 45. When Lindsey was 13, she told me the intriguing story of her 'other mummy', whom she could still recall from her early childhood.

I used to sit in my high chair and my other mummy used to come through the wall and sit by me. She would come through the wall in my bedroom and talk to me about all sorts of things and make me laugh. She looked very much like my mum, only she wasn't.

The identity of the other mummy remained a mystery until at a family party, Lindsay caught sight of a pile of old family photos and pounced on one with delight. 'There she is – my other mummy.' It was her great-granny in an Edwardian wedding dress and she was almost the image of Lindsay's mother, Margaret.

My own daughter, Miranda, who is now 18, can still recall childhood visits from my mother, who died 20 years before her birth. Miranda identified her from a tiny, faded, yellowing photograph.

When Miranda was four or five, she would frequently tell me about Granny Beryl sitting on her bed and that Granny Beryl read her stories.

When she was about seven, she and her older brother Jack, who started my psychic career, came with me to Liverpool when I appeared on the Richard Madeley and Judy Finnegan television show, called *This Morning*. In the only photo Miranda had seen of my mother, she had short curly hair. The make-up artist at the studio put my long wayward hair up into a French pleat at the back of my head. Miranda commented that my hair was exactly like Granny Beryl's. On special occasions, my mother would wear a hairpiece so she could put her hair up in a French pleat, but I had never mentioned this. It was the first time I had worn my hair that way.

My late aunt Ruth, my mother's sister, who lived with me as a child and helped to bring me up, also visits Miranda. My aunt was always very fond of Miranda, who, I think, reminded her of me as a child. On the rare occasions they met, my aunt doted on Miranda.

My aunt had to have one leg amputated below the knee because of circulation problems but never accepted her prosthesis. One night, before her death, my aunt appeared in Miranda's bedroom in her wheelchair. Miranda describes her as a picture on the wall. She told Miranda, 'I'm all right now.' Miranda said that though Aunty Ruth was in the wheelchair, her leg was better. The next day, the news came that she had died.

## Traditional spirit guardians

Some children are guided by a Native North American, or a monk or a nun. These children have often retained their psychic gifts into adulthood. Wendy, who lives in Manchester, England, has seen her guide only once – and he seemed as surprised as she was that she could see him.

> Seven years ago, when I was nine years old, I woke up in the middle of the night for no reason, at about 3 am. As I was on my side, I turned on to my back and saw an American Indian floating over my bed with his eyes closed. Though he was not on my bed, he was sitting down. When he noticed I was awake, he looked shocked, then disappeared. I know it was not a dream, as I got up and turned the light on.

One of saddest cases I have heard of is that of Carol, whom I came across when I was working at the Alister Hardy Research Centre for Religious and Spiritual Experience, ten years ago. As a little girl, Carol used to talk to animals and people whom even her twin sister could not see. When she spoke of seeing a Native North American chief, her parents got so worried that they had her admitted to a mental hospital when she was a teenager. There, she realised that if she was going to get out she had to play by the rules. She no longer mentioned her psychic experiences, although she kept having them. When she was 25, she went to a medium, who told her that she was psychic and had a Native North American guide.

Carol found it hard to forgive her parents for what they did. Although at the time I encountered the case, Carol was holding a responsible job, her parents refused to discuss either what happened or anything to do with her psychic experiences. Hopefully, in the twenty-first century no teenager would be forced into psychiatric treatment for what is a spiritual gift.

## Guardians of the home

Former residents of a house may be sensed or seen after their death, especially if they lived in the house for many years and were happy there. Often, a sensitive child such as Patricia (see page 47) may be able to describe the former owner in detail. Some children strike up a friendship with the spirit, perhaps because the spirit loved children but did not have a family of their own.

When Jamie, who lives in Ayrshire, Scotland, was young, he became attached to an old lady who carried out domestic chores around the home and visited him at night. He was not afraid of her and was surprised that his mother could not see her. Hannah, Jamie's mother, who told me the story, had herself seen the ghost of her grandmother when she was a child.

> We lived in a house built during the 1920s. My husband was away at sea for stretches at a time, and so my younger brother used to stay with me to keep me company. One day, when Jamie was quite young, he came into the living room with £1 and said that the lady had given it to him to buy some sweets. I asked him where the lady was, and he said that she was in the kitchen doing the dishes. We went into the kitchen, and Jamie pointed over to the sink. He said, 'You must be able to see her. She has her hair tied up and glasses. She is looking at you now.'
>
> When I replied that I could see no one, all the dishes on the draining board suddenly flew across the kitchen, the golden retriever ran for his life and Jamie told me I had upset the lady. My brother was petrified.
>
> Jamie had never had an invisible friend, as we were a big family and he had lots of company, but he told me the lady frequently sat in his bedroom between his Smurf and Big Ted by the toy box. There were footsteps on the stairs and doors would open and close by themselves. One morning Jamie told me the lady was over by the sink in the kitchen. It was early and I sent him back to bed and went to make a cup of coffee. I told her she was disrupting our household and that I did not want her around any more. The room felt suddenly cold, but after that Jamie never saw the lady again. When I inquired, I found out that the first inhabitant of the house was a lady who wore glasses and had her hair in a bun. She had lived on her own for years and was very eccentric and had died there.

Ellie lives in Yorkshire, England. She was three when she started talking about the old lady of the house. The family had moved into an old house that needed a great deal of renovation. The old lady never worried Ellie, and they would hold conversations, though only Ellie's replies were audible. When she was 13, the family were going to move. Ellie told the family that the old lady was happy because they had fixed the house. She never spoke of the old lady again. Ellie has a physical disability. I have found that childhood guardians tend to stay with disabled children for much longer.

## When a child sees an angel or spiritual guardian

You are very lucky if your child is blessed by an angelic visitation. Accept what the child tells you without question. A number of children whose experiences I described in this chapter were distressed because their parents ignored or dismissed what was a very precious experience to them. Your child is not abnormal, nor will they necessarily become very religious in later life, but this kind of visitation can be an indication that they are sensitive and may need lots of support in dealing with the everyday world.

Spirit guardians are likewise a gift. If your child speaks of a Native North American or less specific protector, all you need to do is make sure your child has plenty of physical, earthly fun and stimulation to balance their spiritual side. The experience demonstrates that you have a very spiritual child – even if you are not yourself religious. You are lucky, for they will grow up kind and caring.

Contacts from angels and guardians should not spook you, but, regrettably, I have to advocate caution in whom you and your child tell about these encounters. Some people are very worried by such experiences and may fill your child's head with nonsense about scary ghosts. Even professionals may not be comfortable with experiences outside their own particular world view. Hopefully, this situation is improving. You should emphasise to your child that contact with an angel or a guardian is quite normal and nothing to fear but that, like other private family matters, the visits are best shared only within the family. It is a fine balance, and such visitations should never be treated as a secret to be hidden. The family can enquire after the grandparent just as they would anyone else the child has met.

If you have disapproving relatives, make sure they keep any adverse comments well away from the child's ears. Remember that children have bat-like hearing. It can be very hurtful to them to have their experiences belittled by someone less sensitive.

If the guide is a relative, encourage the child to collect pictures and stories about their earthly life. Emphasise the everyday personality of the paranormal visitor, their jokes and foibles. Explain that a grandma or grandfather who cares for the family may well pop back occasionally and that children are more easily able to see them than adults are. Reassure the child that the invisible person is not always watching them but that, like any other welcome visitor, they will call occasionally. Tell the child that if they are too busy to talk, they can say so – if they like, asking the visitor to come back another time. No loving relative would wish to intrude.

If you are not happy about a former inhabitant of your home talking to your child or the child does not want to see the former resident in their bedroom, light a white candle. Sit in front of the candle with your child and encircle the candle with dried lavender, as you do so requesting in a quiet friendly manner that the presence respects that the house is now yours and that you have daily demands to fulfil. Tell them that they are welcome but let them know how often you would prefer them to call and specify times that are suitable. Allow the child to decide what is acceptable and what bothers them and set the limits. Even if you do not believe in the presence, this ritual will set boundaries psychologically and help the child to feel in control.

If you wish, try to identify the presence from the history of the house. If you cannot identify the person, this does not mean that they are not real. Many ghosts are not traceable, and the apparition is still real to the child.

# CHAPTER 6

# Encounters with Fairies and People from Other Dimensions

Even in the modern world, children report seeing fairies, often in the same forms that people described them hundreds of years ago, when life was lived closer to nature. Some children interact directly with fairies. However, many just see nature spirits as they carry on their own existence – some fairies do not welcome contact.

In the popular imagination, fairies are either tiny gossamer-winged Andrew Lang Flower Fairies who can stand on a drop of water without rippling the surface, or the slightly sturdier, moralistic or mischievous advisers of wayward or lost children created by Enid Blyton. Yet, according to legends and reported sightings over hundreds of years (from adults as well as children), fairies are altogether more ambivalent. A small number of fairy encounters have been quite frightening for the child concerned, as fairies are essentially creatures of the natural world that can whip up storms or hurricanes.

## Do fairies and nature spirits exist?

We know that even plants have animate life. Plants radiate light around their physical forms that can be detected by Kirlian photography, a method of capturing auras on film. Plant auras fade when the plant is cut or deprived of water, and if a leaf is removed from a plant, the aura or energy field of the missing part remains.

What is more, plants respond to unspoken threats not only against themselves but also against others of their species. Clive Backster and other researchers working during the 1960s and 70s hooked plants up to polygraph (and later EKG and EEG equipment). They discovered that not only do plants respond to experiences in their environment but they also seem to be able to pick up on people's thoughts. The strongest readings obtained were in reaction to the destruction of living cells, whether of plant, animal or human. The death of living cells, or even the threat of death, caused intense electromagnetic reactions in all the plants present.

Given this knowledge, it may be that the essential life of the natural world can be perceived as fairy forms, especially by children who are very tuned in to other energy frequencies. However, that theory does not fully explain a number of the encounters in this chapter. Therefore we might have to concede that nature essences do exist and share our world, though they may be an altogether more ethereal life form, invisible to the human physical eye. Their bodies may be akin to the spiritual body within humans that survives death and which may be what we see as a ghost.

It is not a comfortable concept for some adults that we are not the only sentient species on earth, but then we cannot fully control nature. These are just speculations – an attempt to explain sightings that do seem to be more than imagination.

## Fairy encounters

I have noticed that a significant proportion of people who saw fairies during their childhood go on to become healers and clairvoyants. It may be simply that these people are more willing to talk about an experience that still is regarded as cranky by many. Often, too, children do not talk about fairy sightings when they are young because they know they will be teased or called babies. It is only in adulthood that such experiences are acknowledged as being more than imagination.

Pat, now aged 50, saw fairies when she was about four, at the bottom of the garden belonging to the old lady who helped to take care of her (Pat's predictive dream is described on page 59).

> It was a big garden with a stream running at the bottom. The fairies were very tiny, dressed in pink gossamer, and used to play around by the stream. I told them my wildest dreams. They used to fly and hover with their tiny wings. I did not tell anyone, as I knew they would have laughed.

Lilian, who lived in Cheshire, England, as a child and is now a healer, was chronically ill with lung problems when she was young. Consequently, she had a great deal of time off school, during which she roamed the countryside. She still has the amazing ability to create wonderful gardens out of wilderness.

> I used to see fairies in our garden in Cheshire, but especially in the woods. They were semi-transparent and tiny with wings. I found myself looking at the little people in shadowy forms. They all looked different according to whether they belonged to a tree, a flower or a bush. Each species was the same colour and even the same texture, and would merge into the tree or flower. I used to sit and watch them for hours. They came in ones and twos and seemed friendly, but they got on with their own world, to which I knew I

was only a visitor, watching, not part. I never told the other children. I knew they would laugh.

Chrissie lives on the Isle of Wight, England, and is a spiritual person, helping to run a New Age store and creating beautiful ceramics. She saw little creatures moving in the grass in her childhood, and can still hear them whispering when she is in the countryside.

Julie recalls that when she was a child, her family had a big garden, and in part of it, where she played, there were little fairy-like spirit friends. To Julie, they were not just pretend. Indeed, she says she has seen them in adult life, especially in a particular place in Devon, England. Her children have also seen them: 'Once, when we were together, we all saw them, when my son was nine and the youngest only about four.' I asked her what they look like. 'They are very fleeting, like butterflies,' she said, 'but not as small, about the size of squirrels.'

## Sharing the experience

Layla and her sister Rhiannon were not country dwellers but grew up in a council house in a northern English industrial town. They both saw the same fairy in their bedroom independently. More than ten years later, both girls are able to recall the details vividly. Layla also saw many other fairies. She told me:

> After being shown the pictures of the Cottingley fairies in a book, I fully expected to see fairies. The fact that I lived on a council estate in Crewe rather than in unspoiled woodland never entered my head. Fairies I wanted, and fairies I got, although not the sweet gossamer creatures I'd pictured.
>
> I've always been a bit of a nature child. I could potter about outside for hours. I was at my happiest when digging around in the muck, climbing trees or playing with bees (I used to let them crawl about on my hands and knees and never got stung). Nature was, and still is, endlessly fascinating to me.
>
> Every time something grabbed my attention, I would see something more intriguing out of the corner of my eye. As my eyes flitted from object to object, something strange would happen. Faces and forms would appear at the sides of my vision. They would appear only for a fraction of a second, and when I looked again, they wouldn't be there. These faces and forms soon became familiar to me. I never thought to question them until years later.
>
> There were three distinct types, although I did occasionally see one I didn't recognise. The first type was the only one to worry me slightly. It was two-legged and had no body and an eyeless head, a little like a swan's beak (but it didn't seem to have a mouth; its head was just in that shape). Its legs were like horses' legs but much thinner. It was a cloudy grey-brown colour and much taller

than me. It was so tall in fact that I'd never see the top and bottom half of it in one glance.

My grandfather has two plaques on the wall. An artist friend cast them for him out of metal. They show two creatures very similar to what I saw in the woods. The similarity struck me one day, and I asked him what the creatures were. He replied: 'They're the things you see out of the corner of your eyes when you're alone in the woods.'

The second type was something I called tree men. These were very strange indeed. For a second it would look as if somebody was entering or leaving through an invisible door on a tree trunk. The 'somebody' would be very indistinct and transparent but definitely there. On one occasion, a head poked out of a tree, saw me and promptly disappeared back inside.

The third main type of fairy that I saw was closest to the butterfly-winged classic variety. It was small, about the size of a Barbie doll. It seemed very brittle, as if it was made of dry twigs. It would always be a lighter shade of the colours of the plants around it. Its eyes were huge and black, it had no nose and if it had a mouth I didn't notice one. It would appear to be made out of a plant, with leaves and other foliage growing out of it. This fairy would always peek out from under something, although I did see one silhouetted against the sky once.

My sister Rhiannon and I were chatting recently about the house we grew up in. We used to share the tiny front bedroom. We'd never spoken about this before, as she was so young when we lived there (she's seven years younger than me). The front bedroom was, as my sister put it, 'weird'. She shuddered to herself and then went on to tell me a few strange things that happened to her She described the exact same thing I saw for several nights running. We both saw a tiny figure standing behind the curtain early in the morning.

I remember this so clearly because I thought my mother had put a doll behind the curtain as a joke. I snatched the curtain back and there was nothing to be seen. Nothing to cast that sort of a shadow on to the window either. When the curtain fell back again it was gone. My sister said that she used to see it from her cot, and she told me that its hair seemed to be in a kind of loose Afro style that fitted in perfectly with what I saw.

Lots of strange things happened in that front bedroom. Among these were a goblin-type creature running across the floor just as I was waking up, my name being whispered very loudly and distinctly behind me as I played in the otherwise empty room and the constant feeling that there was somebody in the corner of the room (not a bad feeling but not a very comfortable one either!).

Rhiannon independently confirmed this story.

I was the youngest, so anything about fairies was put down to my imagination. Stories usually resulted in, 'You're tired; go to bed', so I wasn't one to mention them. There was only one fairy I remember clearly. She looked like a doll with a big floating dress on. She had really huge, frizzy, shoulder-length hair and she was really pretty, very pale though. All she did was pace up and down on my windowsill. The room my sister and I shared was the scariest, and we saw loads of weird stuff in there, usually around the window. The fairy looked at me once. I was really interested, but as soon as I got up to touch her, she was gone.

## The Cottingley fairies: the only scientific evidence for fairies?

The most famous case of 'fairies at the bottom of the garden' is probably the Cottingley affair, over which there is still controversy more than 70 years later.

The following is, as far as I can ascertain, the true version of events, although a reviewer from an American fairy website took issue with a similar account published in my *Complete Guide to Faeries and Magical Beings* (see page 187). My account is based on discussions and correspondence with the most experienced Cottingley researcher, Joe Cooper, who interviewed the girls involved when they were much older. Therefore I will stick with this account.

In 1917, cousins Frances Griffiths, aged 11, and Elsie Wright, aged 16, claimed to have played with fairies in a glen at Cottingley, in the Yorkshire Dales (in northern England), and to have produced photographs of them that baffled experts in both photography and the paranormal, including Kodak and Sir Arthur Conan Doyle, the creator of Sherlock Holmes and an ardent spiritualist. One photograph showed a group of fairy-like figures dancing in front of a girl, another a winged gnome-like creature near a girl's beckoning hand.

Some 60 years later, the cousins admitted that four of the photographs had been faked. They had made cut-outs of fairies and placed them in the glen. However, this was not the end of the story, because, according to Frances, they did take one genuine photograph. She told Joe Cooper: 'It was a wet Saturday afternoon, and we were just mooching about with our cameras, and Elsie had nothing prepared. I saw these fairies building up in the grasses and just aimed the camera and took a photograph.'

Elsie insisted that all the photographs were fakes. However, along with Frances, she claimed that there actually were fairies. The reason they had faked the pictures was to prove to doubting adults that the fairy folk did exist. (Many of the so-called 'child frauds' in psychism result from demands to prove an experience true.) It would not be surprising if, in later life, Elsie was tired of the pressure of upholding the truth of her experiences. I have heard that Frances also went back on her story at one point, but I have no reason to believe that she told Joe anything other than the truth.

### Other nature essences

Not every child sees nature essences in the form of fairies. Susan, from Southampton, England, had a gnome as a friend.

> When I was a child, he lived in a greenhouse and was called Johnny Morris. I can still see him. He was small with blond hair and a fair complexion. I asked my mother, and she cannot remember me saying that he spoke at all. She recalls that he lived in the left-hand side of the greenhouse that was in the garden of our home. As I am writing this to you, I can feel the warmth of the greenhouse and the smell of tomatoes that were growing. There was also a very tiny stone wall with metal pillars. The tops came off and you could look inside. They were hollow. This was at the front of the house. I am sure Johnny used to play there as well. I am convinced he was more like a gnome than a fairy. I was about three when I saw him.

Gnomes are earth spirits and are often associated with gardens where ceramic gnomes are kept as symbols of good fortune and prosperity.

### Frightening fairies

The strangest fairy account I have come across is that of two women, both called Nicola, who met as adults. Both had had identical fairy experiences as children. Nicky, who lives on the Isle of Wight, England, told me:

> As a child, I quite frequently saw cartoon-like figures giving off their own light. They were not living creatures but animated. There were sparks and then they appeared. They would fly away and come back. There were little men with big eyes, pulling horrible faces. Then there were stereotyped witches with warts and big noses and pointed chins. Some were one foot [30 centimetres] wide, down to 7 inches [17 centimetres].
>
> Some were tiny and beautiful little witches with curly black hair, black pointed hats and broomsticks. They were really beautiful. The nasty outweighed the good. The nice ones went back and forward.
>
> The experience occurred on ten or more occasions. Mum said they weren't there, but they were everywhere. So I pointed to one. She said we should tell it to go away and it would disappear. We found them and got rid of them one by one. But they still came back several times afterwards.

Nikki, the second Nicola, now living in Hertfordshire, England, also described her parallel experience for me:

When I was eight or nine it was a traumatic time, as Dad was leaving. A humming sound and the little figures would come towards me. I hated the noise and would hold my ears. The noise faded as they went away. I saw them coming towards me laughing, and they would change colour and face. They were circular, different sizes, and had faces with different colours around them. They got bigger and louder as they got nearer. I shared a room with my sisters and would wake them.

The creatures would be by the curtains and they moved and shot across the room. It just stopped after a couple of years. Some of the faces were nice and some were horrible. They made ugly faces at me and poked their tongues out. My mother would not believe me.

Fairy energies manifest in different ways. I have come across other accounts of unpleasant experiences, including one I have recalled in the chapter on Frightening Psychic Experiences (see page 147). On the whole, indoor nocturnal fairy experiences tend to be less pleasant, maybe because the energies have got trapped inside, like an insect that cannot find the window. Because these entities have distinctive appearances, I am convinced that they are more than the free-floating psychic energies that I have also written about in Chapter 9.

Andrew, who lives in Portsmouth, England, saw fairies in the unlikely setting of a school corridor and described similar phenomena.

One fairy had a green light and one a blue light. They were the size of the palm of my hand. The fairy beings were in the centre of the light that became paler the further away the light was from them. They went by very quickly, one in front of the other, as if they were playing tag.

## Other nasty nature spirits

Ivy, like Nikki (see above), had to face her fears alone. What she described were stereotypical goblins. Goblins are small, strong, ugly and often spiteful creatures that usually roam in bands and live in dark underground places or deep forests. They are known in legend for terrifying children. I found Ivy's account in an archive at the Alister Hardy Research Centre when I was researching children's experiences there. Ivy wrote of her terror to Alister Hardy:

I think I would have been seven years old when I lived in sheer terror in our farmhouse. It was quite a lonely house, way up in the hills, directly on the Pennine Chain. I never told my parents because they (and I) would have said I was dreaming.

But it is only these last years I realise that these horrible, thin, wizened, toothless, spiky, grey-haired and some young, ill-fed

> people were actually in my bedroom, which was built on to the Elizabethan part of the old farmhouse.
>
> They mocked and laughed and leered at me from behind the wardrobe, the wash stand, and sometimes came close to the bed. My mother bought me an iron tonic, for she realised I had dark rings under my eyes.
>
> I was finally moved from my bedroom because she thought it might be too cold for me. I have never forgotten the people. I actually lost weight. It was a kind of torment, as if something was trying to break me down.
>
> As a child I had the feeling when the terror stopped of being the winner, as if I had conquered a kind of fear, something my mother and father could not do for me. Even at this early age, there was the knowledge that I must face it myself. That was 50 years ago, and it gave me a lot of strength

The late Vivien Greene, wife of the author Graham Greene, talked to me at her home in Oxfordshire, England, and corresponded with me a great deal about her numerous psychic experiences both as a child and as a mother (see also page 34). She described how she and her son had simultaneously seen a dark elf in her son's bedroom.

> When my son Francis was between three and four, we were living in a house in Oxford. Francis was sleeping in a bed with drop-sided cot rails on either side. One evening I was putting him to sleep when he suddenly became distressed and told me, 'I don't like the little man at the bottom of my bed.'
>
> In a flash, I saw momentarily what my son was seeing, the top half of an elf or gnome with a malevolent spiteful face, standing there. Just as quickly, the creature was gone and there was just a pile of blankets at the end of the bed.

It is very common for children and mothers to share experiences, for their psyches are not fully separated during the early years of a child's life. Indeed, mothers often re-awaken their own psychic powers when they have children. This may partly explain why women who are mothers sometimes more easily see fairies and ghosts in the presence of their children.

### Fairies and alien encounters

Why have I included alien encounters with fairies? Because extra-terrestrial and fairy encounters share a number of significant points in common.

While fairies have their magic rings, aliens are increasingly being implicated in the sudden appearance of crop circles. With both fairy and alien encounters, lights may appear in the sky. Indeed, some modern UFO abductees locate the place to which they were taken by extra-terrestrials as under ground or under water, with brilliant light shining up from the depths of the water. This parallels descriptions of fairy realms in Celtic literature.

Extra-terrestrials reported include tall, noble Nordic types; beings very like statuesque opalescent fairies, as described in Celtic mythology; and – the most commonly reported kind – 'greys', who share physical characteristics with goblins. Reports would suggest that, like fairies, greys are often amoral, curious rather than empathic towards humans and as capable of behaving with cruelty or indifference as with kindness.

Let me give you some examples of the parallels before going on to discuss children and extra-terrestrial encounters.

On 10 December 1954, at a place called Chico-Cerro de las Tres Torres, in Venezuela, dwarf-like hairy beings, no more than four feet (120 centimetres) tall were reported to have landed in a spacecraft and attacked two hunters. From France, too, at around this time, came accounts of goblin-like creatures attacking people, mocking them and dancing around. In 1955, in one of the earliest reported direct encounters with extra-terrestrial beings in the US, five tiny goblin-like creatures with dark, wrinkled pigmented skin and large ears and eyes were seen by a family outside their farm in Kentucky. The farmers shot at one of the creatures, but the bullet fell off it with a metallic sound. When a family member went outside to investigate, one of the creatures touched his hair with a silvery hand. These extra-terrestrials became known as the Hopkinsville Goblins.

Some researchers believe that both fairies and extra-terrestrials are creatures of other dimensions that exist on different energy frequencies from humans. In earlier times, stories of fairy abductions may have been descriptions of the same phenomenon as modern alien kidnappings but were understood in the pre-technological terminology of the period. Whatever the truth of this theory, there are fascinating parallels. What is more, it is arrogant of humans to believe that we are the only intelligent life force in the cosmos.

### The Star children

Mary Rodwell of the Australian Close Encounter Resource Network has recently described research into a new breed of highly intelligent children known as Star children. Star children are described as being like small adults in a child's body. They possess highly evolved psychic powers, a recall of past worlds in other galaxies and an amazing ability with technology from an early age. They are more prevalent among parents who have reported experiencing alien abductions. An explanation could be that there is extra-terrestrial genetic input or bio-engineering that enhances the capacity of the human genes during the abduction.

You will find a list of books on extra-terrestrial encounters and Star children on page 187. There is also an excellent article by Mary Rodwell, Principal of the Australian Close Encounter Resource Network (ACERN), which includes some fascinating case studies. Her contact details can be found on page 187. Rodwell cites the work of Richard Boylan, psychologist, clinical hypnotherapist and secretary of the Academy of Clinical Close Encounter Therapists (ACCET) in America, who coined the name Star children (also known as *homo noeticus*). She calls these super-children 'new kids on the block'. I am keeping an open mind and will follow this research for future editions of this book.

In response to an appeal I made in the *Vancouver Sun,* I have been sent one account of a Star child by a parent in British Columbia, Canada. Graham Conway, of UFO British Columbia has also published this account on the internet. I have promised total anonymity for the sake of the child but can attest that the account is totally genuine. The girl is now nine years old. I reproduce this report with thanks to the parents and to Graham.

UFO British Columbia received an e-mail stating that on July 1st 2001 Francis spotted a UFO at 9 pm on her way to bed. She claims that it was rotating and beaming down a light that apparently was shone in her direction. As this witness is six years old, it was her father who made us aware of these facts.

A lengthy phone conversation plus a later meeting between this parent and myself resulted in an opportunity to talk to the young lady. Of particular interest was a strange dream that she could recall in detail and had illustrated and described in her own words. Bearing in mind that this young lady is not saturated in UFO hype, I have to admit to being surprised at some of the statements she makes and relates in a very matter-of-fact manner.

We felt that this account was sufficiently noteworthy that we should share it with our readers so that they may be aware that we have here a very bright child who is possibly at the start of a lifetime of further adventures.

Francis reproduces drawings of flying saucers, cargo, an alien lady and a rocket ship. Then she draws more pictures and writes: 'The alien body is as tall as a doorway. She said to a person that they were going to take over the world and she would be leading taking over North America. She switched brains with the lady she was talking with.'

Then Francis describes a picture she drew of 'grey and black disks that are flying saucers and those table like things are stands. Those squares are boxes and cargo, being loaded on the disks. The rocket ship is a large white cylinder with a red triangle on top.'

Finally she says: 'There was a lab where they mixed different cells and body parts and colours and sounds to turn people into different creatures. She said that if I didn't watch out that would happen to me!'

Francis's father, Tom, filled in the background for me. 'After working through this with Graham, I recall a similar dream with a big lady in it, much like what Francis experienced. I was only six at the time, and nobody listened so it became a repressed memory that now is clear as day. I'd like to be able to understand who the big lady is.'

Her father says that Francis has been in a gifted writing program for three years now and reads at an adult level; at the end of this year she was selected as gifted in maths as well.

In Berkshire, England, I came across another alien experience. James was nine when I collected this account, for the first edition of this book. According to his mother, Carolyn, the incidents started when James was about four-and-a-half. He wasn't having trouble at school or at home. Carolyn persuaded him to tell me about his magical land. James was reluctant to talk, and, as a former teacher, I am usually very aware of when a story is made up. So why was this different? It was to do with the matter-of-fact way in which the child, James, described another world. The experiences also persisted long after a child would normally have forgotten about such things. Imagination? You decide.

James told me he has a home on another planet where he goes where he cannot sleep. He is very reluctant to talk about this world outside the family, because people tease him, so he tends to clam up. His five-year-old sister insisted that he has taken her there and that the trees were red.

According to Carolyn, James is an insomniac. James says that on his planet the people stay awake at night and go to bed by day, so he is able to go there at night.

Perhaps the most surprising thing is that James is not a galactic hero but has a house and a mother and father in this other world to whom he is an only child. He lives there in a remarkably ordinary house. In the garden bananas grow on trees. The leaves are yellow and the bananas are brown when they are ripe. James says:

I have my own small house in the garden. The houses are red like clay, except the walls are completely flat with no bumps. Usually every home has a computer and my Dad just shoots stars and things, and my mum does the housework with computerised gadgets. I don't go to school. We go to the park sometimes. It is like the local park except it's got a slide like a spiral that spins round.

I do not play with anyone really. It's always light there. I look at the clock and come back when I think it's teatime. That gets me back to this other house at 4 o'clock. Then I sleep till morning.

James said he gets to Planet X, as he calls it, in a small spacecraft that is operated by remote control. There is room for three. He recalls when his sister came along, she was naughty and picked some apples that were orange but had stalks like ours. He says: 'I think I might stop going there some day, but I do not think I would be sad.'

James would be an adult by now. Unfortunately, I lost touch with his family. James also had snatches of past life recall, which I have described on page 137.

### How to encourage fairy encounters

Encourage your child to spend time in the open air, playing in woodlands, on the seashore or in the park on family outings. Contact with the natural world on any level is very positive, providing a welcome antidote to the over-stimulation of theme parks (and is much cheaper).

On family trips, walk quietly with the child so that they can observe wildlife, birds and small animals. Point out the different qualities of flowers and trees. Talk about the kinds of beings that, according to folklore, live in them and tell your child about some of the ideas about fairies and nature essences from different traditions. (For books on this subject, see page 187.) If you do not know much about the countryside, read up on flowers and trees so that you help your child to identify the different varieties. Children of all ages enjoy doing this. If you live in a town, visit an arboretum or wildlife garden. Even quite a young child will sit motionless for a few minutes, watching plants as they sway in the breeze.

If you have a garden, find a place where the child can create a miniature secret garden. If you are handy with wood or have a willing relative, make a simple playhouse or treehouse out of wood (so much more satisfying than the garish, overpriced, plastic variety). Alternatively, help the child to make a temporary den with old blankets.

Show your child pictures from old-fashioned fairy books. There has been a revival in these, with plenty of cheap editions available. Read traditional fairy stories and fairy lore together. These are part of our heritage, but they can get lost in the computer-simulated, television-orientated world that bombards the child with images but does not encourage their own imagination.

### When a child has a fairy encounter

Children can be reluctant to talk about seeing fairies, but on walks together you can explain how the rustling in the leaves sounds like fairy voices. They may open up and tell you what they have seen or heard. Help the child to draw, paint or record their own fairy tales and images. You may be surprised how even a young child's description matches that of traditional folklore.

If your child is frightened by small beings, either indoors or out, take their words seriously. If the child can see the beings, ask them to point to the figures. Then, even if you cannot see them, you can help the child to send them away. You may need to do this several times.

If the beings are indoors – even if you are convinced they exist only in the child's imagination – open the windows and doors with the child to let them out where they belong. One sceptical parent was amazed by a whole lot of moths appearing apparently from nowhere and heading out of the child's bedroom window. It stopped his child's night-time visits by scary elves, imagined or not.

## When a child has an extra-terrestrial encounter

Try to monitor the television and cinema viewing of even older children to avoid the nastier alien movies that can lead to nightmares.

If your child does talk about dreams of aliens, listen sympathetically, especially if they are frightened. Reassure your child that no one will take them away. Sometimes fears of aliens can be a way for the child to express deep-seated fears of being alienated from the family or friends or being sent away. They may also have a need to share fears of abduction by earthly strangers.

If the dreams occur often, suggest that the child makes friends with the aliens in their dreams. Encourage them to keep a journal of their encounters. This is a good way of dealing with any fears and – who knows? – you may find that your child's academic performance improves dramatically.

You may recall having similar dreams when you were young but that you had forgotten. Be wary who you tell, as some less scrupulous media organisations may exploit you. If you want to contact a UFO organisation, be very careful to find out all about the organisation before revealing any details and insist on a confidentiality clause.

I personally would not allow anyone to hypnotise my child, and you should be as cautious of such therapists as you are of any practitioner, even if they have medical qualifications.

# CHAPTER 7

# Out-of-body and Near-death Experiences

Out-of-body experiences are a feature of childhood. Young children often talk of spontaneously floating or flying downstairs. As children become older and move towards adolescence, they may become aware of the power to leave their bodies and travel where they will. The relatively large number of teenage accounts of out-of-body travel suggests that this is one way that they test their limits and assert power they may not feel or be able to express in their daily lives. For this reason, it is helpful to adolescents to have a sensible but understanding adult to be able to talk to, as they may frighten themselves, especially if they try to induce experiences.

We do not know whether out-of-body experiences are mind travel or the actual journeying of the spirit body that we all possess. The fact that some people's double, called a doppelganger, is reported at a time when they are astrally travelling suggests that there may be actual travel involved. Astral comes from the Latin *astra,* meaning 'star', and is a common term for travelling upwards.

In this chapter I will also investigate the much rarer but related near-death experience. This occurs when a very sick child or teenager momentarily clinically dies or is rendered unconscious, perhaps in an accident or operation. They travel along a dark tunnel to a beautiful place where there are flowers, music and sometimes a deceased relative waiting. Invariably, they are sent back by their relative to finish their earthly life. Almost all near-death experiences, although independently reported, are remarkably similar.

### Our spirit or etheric form

Many researchers into spiritual energies believe that we possess within our physical body a spirit or etheric body. This is hypothesised to be the part of us – our essential soul – that survives after death. It has been described clairvoyantly and also by children either as a silver essence or as a double of our physical body at its peak.

It is often said that we are all spiritual beings in an earthly body. Children and teenagers are still sufficiently connected to their inner spiritual nature to be able to operate within their spiritual body without the complicated techniques most adults need for astral projection. Of course, our spirit and earthly bodies occupy the same space while we are alive. However, the inner body is not packed with flesh and organs but is altogether lighter and brighter, made of pure energy. This inner spirit body is a mass of swirling rainbow colours. Because it is so filled with energy, it extends beyond the limits of the physical body as a rainbow energy field. This external energy field is called our aura, or psychic energy field, and may be seen by children and clairvoyants.

Jean, a healer from Surrey, England, told me that when her young daughter was small she used to play a game of making her astral body run down the steps in front of her physical body.

Esther, from London, England is only three but talks about colours around strangers' as well as family members' heads. These colours, she says, change according to whether they are happy, sad or worried.

## Floating or flying experiences in early childhood

A considerable number of adults recall having experienced the sensation of floating downstairs as children, a power that seems to fade at about the age of five. Mary, who lives in Leeds, England, reported an experience that is typical of the many accounts I have collected of this childhood phenomenon:

> It happened quite spontaneously when I was about three. I took off from the top of the stairs and floated below, alighting gently at the bottom.

Jane, from Worcestershire, England, described how, at the age of eight:

> I floated upstairs and down again. The staircase turned at the top of the house, and there was a banister along the wall. It was a wonderful sensation, and I floated back up again. I felt so powerful. Then I fell from top to bottom and never tried again. Mum didn't believe me at the time, but now she understands.

Clare who lives in Herefordshire, England, says that she often floated head-first down the stairs in dreams as a child.

> Once, though, I actually found myself at the bottom of the stairs. I wasn't hurt, but I was really frightened. Nan and Granddad were in the sitting room with my mum, and I can remember hiding behind my mum on the settee.

Cicely, from Hampshire, England says:

> I went to the staircase outside my bedroom door and took off, gliding gently down the stairs, head-first I think. It was daylight, a summer evening. I think I was five years old. In those days one was sent to bed at set times, regardless of the light. The next night,

I again went to the head of the stairs, but it did not work. I was extremely disappointed. Flying through the air was a wonderful sensation. If this was a dream, it was certainly no ordinary one.

Lesley, who lives near Heathrow Airport, in England, said she could remember floating downstairs as a child. 'When did it stop?' I asked her. 'When we moved into a flat,' she replied.

Though some psychoanalysts interpret floating and flying as having deep psychological significance, it can perhaps be more simply regarded as a child testing the limits of their powers. As they get older, these are limited by the awareness of the physical limitations on what is possible.

My own experience of floating downstairs was rather more frightening. Many years later I still have nightmares about it. However, it was not until I became aware of psychic phenomena that I understood what had happened to me. Indeed, as I write about this experience, I am aware of details that I had buried resurfacing.

It happened when I was about three. My family lived in a small terraced house in Birmingham, England, and there was an almost vertical flight of stairs in the narrow hallway between what we called the front room and the living room. Upstairs, I slept in the back bedroom, which had a very deep walk-in cupboard. In the cupboard were all kinds of old objects, such as my mother's wedding dress, huge paper parasols and a pull-along wicker basket that I kept my dolls in, and which for some reason I called Cooper.

Every night when I was small, if I had to cross the bottom of the stairs (there was no light), I was aware of a cross old woman standing on the small landing at the top of the stairs. I could not move and could not call out but was pulled up the stairs. I never touched the stairs as I ascended very fast. I desperately tried to resist the magnetic pull of the old woman, for I knew that if she took me into the cupboard, I would never be able to escape. Then suddenly I was free and would either float or fall down the stairs. I would run into the living room and be terrified to go to bed. I had no bruises, but the experience seemed – and still seems – totally real. I never talked about it or asked who the old woman was.

It was not until many years later, when I was a mother myself, that I saw a small photograph of my grandmother, who died ten years before I was born. She was the old woman who had pulled me upstairs. I am not certain of the details of the story, but the gist of it is that she hated her own children and would give away their toys while they were at school. She had coerced my mother into an unhappy marriage with the son of a friend across the road. This was purely so that my mother would stay in the family home with her new husband, and my grandmother could live there. Even as I write, 50 years later, I can see the stairs.

In my case there was a lot of tension at home in my early childhood, though it was all kept from me, so maybe I was picking up on some of the free-floating anger and fear.

## Classic out-of-body experiences in middle childhood

For some children, early floating experiences develop into full out-of-body travel that may continue into adulthood.

Lesley, who floated downstairs regularly (see page 106), had her first full-blown out-of-body experience when she was only seven. She told me:

> It was a sunny day. I was sitting with my back against a bush. Suddenly, I was in the red tree, sitting up there. I knew I was there. It was a copper beech tree, and I could see myself sitting on the ground in the distance quite far away. I was very happy, hiding from people up there. There were lots of people around, because there was a party at our house. Eventually, I got down from the tree and went back in my body.

Lesley enjoyed her experience – 'It made me feel good,' she says. It also served as a means of escape from all the people she didn't want to mix with. She says she has had two other out-of-body experiences, one as a teenager and one when she was 20. Each time it was a specific sound that seemed to trigger off the experience. 'When I was very young,' she says, 'the first time, it was the sound of wheels. I think it was a pram going past.'

Alison, who now lives in Scotland, could move from place to place just by thinking about it when she went to school. But she did not actually fly. She described the movement as lifting up, vibrating and travelling like a hovercraft just above the ground. She recalled two incidents in detail. Once, she wanted to hear what some children were saying on the other side of the playground, so she lifted herself up and went over there. She says they were not aware of her being there, but she could hear their words quite clearly. On another occasion, she remembers standing against a tree, playing hide and seek. Again, she lifted herself up and went to see where the other children were hiding. The experiences stopped when the family moved to Scotland, when she was ten.

Some psychologists argue that out-of-body experiences result from unfulfilled wishes projected on to a second life that the subject can control – a sort of super-self! This would be especially attractive to children. For quite young children, an out-of-body-type trance can be a way of escaping from a reality in which they may feel rejected.

Karl who lives in Lancashire, England, gave this description:

> I withdrew from the melée of a football game with friends and walked to the school gates. I started to feel sleepy – as if I was

dropping into a trance. A soft breeze was blowing against my face. The evening was soft and warm. The warmth was more and more intense. I attempted to wake myself from this dream-like state but found I could not. Suddenly, I found myself above – way above – the others and my own physical body, calmly observing my friends. As I remained there, 30 feet [10 metres] above the ground, as if floating, I was in no way aware of being attached to a physical body or physical existence. It was as if part of my mind had decided to take its leave. I sensed a strange kind of dominance over my earthbound companions. I am up here; you are down there. At this, I felt even more satisfied, complete, above human understanding and knowledge.

Suddenly, one of my friends shouted my name. The voice that replied so angrily, 'Shut up!' seemed more distant, yet it was my voice, I am certain. My friend called out a second time. Suddenly, I leapt back into my body. Then I remained rooted to the spot, dazed and confused.

Karl says that he was unfit. Perhaps this made him feel inferior to his friends, since young boys tend to scorn weakness at sport.

## Keeping the gift

Sue, from Manchester, England, works in television. She has had out-of-body experiences since she was a child, and these have continued throughout her adult life. She told me:

My experiences began when I was nine and my family was living in a three-bedroom flat in Manchester. I used to share a bed with my sister, who was 12 months older. I would go to bed and then be aware that my eyes were open and I was in a corner of the ceiling. I could see my sister and my own body below on the bed. This happened five nights out of seven, and I was terrified because I could not control the experience.

I never told anyone because I was afraid that they would laugh or think I was going mad. The experiences stopped when I was 13 and began to menstruate but came back when I was 17. However, I was no longer afraid because I found I could control my body and float where I wanted to. I never went outside the room. I was totally relaxed and felt like marshmallow.

For Tracey, a clairvoyant and author from Suffolk, England, astral travel began when she was quite young. Her ability, like Sue's, has never left her. She told me:

I have been psychic all my life and clearly recall memories of when I was a baby and a toddler. Since a young child, I remember leaving my body when I fell asleep and travelling in the astral world. I was never frightened and always felt protected from any harm or evil.

As a teenager, my abilities started to develop more. I started to see and hear spirits and was aware that I was able to leave my body at night. In my out-of-body state I could not only see and hear spirits but I became one of them.

I do not recall any specific memories of where I went, but I always hovered above my body upon return to it, just before waking and looking down at myself asleep on the bed. Then I fell down into it, from a great height, and woke with a jolt, with my stomach in a knot, as it feels when one has suddenly fallen.

Sometimes as a child I also saw in my bedroom an elderly lady dressed in Victorian clothes with her hair in a bun. She often walked around my bedroom and once sat next to my bed and hugged me. I saw her whilst out of my body and still felt her warm touch upon having returned to it after waking, although her touch disappeared the more I regained consciousness.

## Frightening out-of-body experiences

Out-of-body experiences such as Lesley and Karl's are very empowering – and Sue, too, found that she enjoyed the sensation of astral travelling once she could control it. However, an out-of-body experience can be terrifying if it occurs at night and the child feels out of control.

Norma, from Liverpool, England, is in her seventies but can still remember an out-of-body experience that terrified her at the age of 11.

I went to bed as usual. I was not ill or anything. That night I awoke and I had left my body and was looking down on myself sleeping from somewhere near the ceiling. It was an old house with high ceilings. From the ceiling protruded a hand – a right hand, and a man's because there was part of a shirt cuff. I took hold of the hand. It began to draw me upwards, and a voice I did not recognise as male or female said, 'Come with me.'

I said, 'No, I can't come,' and let go of the hand. The next moment I was in my body again, gasping for breath and desperate to get enough air in my lungs. For a few seconds I really thought I would die, but gradually I recovered. The picture today is as vivid as when it happened.

Sylvia, who lives in Norfolk, England, also feared for a moment that she was going to die.

It happened when I was 11. I was lying in my bed and trying to get to sleep. Then I could see my own body lying on the bed and my sister, who was in the bed next to mine. I didn't float to the ceiling but stayed suspended between the beds. But the strange thing was that I felt as if I was a mass of black dots. Next thing I knew, I was back in my body. I told my mother I had thought I was dying. She gave me some brandy to calm me down.

Were these bad dreams or did the children really leave their bodies? Many out-of-body experiences do happen at night or first thing in the morning. This may be because the conscious mind is at its least active at these times, thus removing constraints on psychic activity.

Sharing their fears with a parent can reassure the child that they won't just float away from their body and not get back.

### Experiments that go wrong

Some children and young people who experiment with out-of-body experiences find ways of controlling them, and so succeed in transforming them into something very positive. However, others only succeed in frightening themselves. Paranormal sensations induced out of curiosity can be too much for a delicate teenage psyche. On the whole, I would advocate leaving psychic development until adulthood except under controlled learning conditions.

Gordon, from Clydeside, Scotland, frightened himself with an out-of-body experience when he was 14 (although in the long term his experience gave him a great sense of security). For a year he had been experimenting with his dreams, trying to control them and leave his body.

> My mother used to call me every morning in time for breakfast and work (I started at the local docks on my fourteenth birthday). One trick I played on her was to rattle my shoes under my bed and shout 'I'm coming.' This particular morning, I must have dropped back into a doze. My mother lost her temper. She came upstairs and gave a sharp knock on my door. 'Gordon, get out of bed!'
>
> Immediately, I found myself suspended above my body and bed, about one foot [30 centimetres] in distance. I clearly saw my body on the bed below. The situation was very real – indeed, more real than most of life's experiences. 'God, I'm dead!' I thought. I embraced my body below on the bed, thinking, 'I've got to get back.' I hugged the body with my arms. I remember looking up at the ceiling with relief. I was back in my body again. At the same time, I could feel my heart pounding fast and I remember my mother entering the room and remarking, 'What on earth's wrong with you?'
>
> The effect of my experience was an overwhelming sense of security. Life does not stop here on earth. The only problem has been getting anyone to believe me.

Alan, from Bedfordshire, England, explains how he scared not himself but his sister:

> When I was ten, I was given permission to stay up late to listen to the radio. The time was about 9.30 pm. I remember clearly thinking it must be possible for your spirit/soul to detach itself

from the physical body and roam free. I sat still. I don't know for how long. Then I realised all was still and silent, and I was truly free. I was not frightened and decided to look at myself. This I did, and in fact was studying myself hard when suddenly I was conscious of a movement on my left-hand side, and the kitchen door opened. My sister, Eleanor, walked in. She looked at my physical body and screamed. Without any effort on my part, I found myself whole again.

I asked my sister if she was all right. She was very upset and told me she thought I was dead. She said I was totally empty, like a shell. I was going to tell her, but she became pretty angry and accused me of trying to frighten her. She threatened to tell my parents, but I reached a pact with her, though I did not tell her what had really happened.

## Flying in dreams

I have worked as dream analyst on four series of the UK television reality show *Big Brother*. The most interesting dream occurred in the celebrity series and belonged to Melinda Messenger, a former model who has become a successful TV personality in the UK. Melinda described the childhood dream to her housemates:

I was on top of a hill and it was like in an old-fashioned battle, with spears being thrown and arrows shooting everywhere. Suddenly, I could see this spear coming towards me, this arrow. I thought, 'Okay, jump. This is my dream. Jump!' and I jumped. I thought, 'This is great. I can control it ... Right, well, I'll fly down the hill.' So I flew down to the bottom. Then I ate a huge bag of candies, every one of them.

You can read more about this and other *Big Brother* dreams in my *Modern Book of Dream Interpretation* (see page 186).

The ability to control events in dreams is known as lucid dreaming. This technique is usually lost in adulthood but can be relearnt. Debbie, who is a web designer and lives in central France, described lucid dreams in which she could travel where she wanted.

When I was between the age of about 11 and 18 I could easily control my dreams. I would have the most wonderful flying dreams – one in particular where I went straight up, out through a roof, up through the sky and into space. I had a brief look at the earth from above, got a bit scared and came straight back down again. I used to find it very easy to drift off into sleep choosing that night's adventure before I fell asleep. I could do practically anything. I have walked under water, finding it easy to breathe, exploring the bottom of lakes and finding secret rooms.

Debbie's flying experiences were also triggered by nightmares.

I used to have nightmares, mainly of my family members killing me in all manner of ways. I have been pushed downstairs and suffocated with a pillow by my lovely brother (who I adore). He has also shot me with a bow and arrow (along with a couple of others in my family!). I have been stabbed, shot, drowned.

But sometimes in my dreams I have been killed by complete strangers as well. I've died in all of them, and when I died it all went black, then I would lie there thinking, 'Well, if now I'm dead and still thinking and aware, I can go and do whatever I like.' So I would get up and go off and do things in the dream. A bit bizarre really.

Then the dreams progressed to me being chased by some form of danger each night. When it became too close (and very often I would realise I was dreaming), I would just launch into the air and fly as an escape. Once I had lost the pursuant, I would think, 'This is great. Let's go exploring.' So I would just go off flying and see where it took me.

Once I just went locally, over the local fruit gardens, just near where I lived, following the river. It was all very vivid, and, as far as I could tell, the landscape was all as it should be, not distorted in any way like dreams can do. I used to fly in and through houses. The one where I went up into space started at a big party in a huge house. In the dream I wasn't enjoying the party, so I went upstairs and was looking down over a balcony. Then I just decided to go up through the roof. I hovered around above the trees and got the idea to go up really high. It was very vivid. I remember looking at the stars, and then I was looking down at the earth. But I got chicken because of the height so came back down.

I have always remembered my dreams, and they are always very vivid. I dream a lot every night. The floating dreams where I was in water were good. I would usually be in the throes of drowning, realise that this must be a dream, and then deliberately breathe in. Once I had done that, I could breathe under water and would go exploring. I remember once walking along the bottom of a lake and finding a metal room.

The last flying dream I had, which was after a gap of many years, was about ten years ago. I was being chased and remembered to fly. I got beyond being chased. Then I thought how I would really like to go and fly over the Acropolis. I was flying along. I saw the sun coming up over the distant horizon and the Acropolis in the distance. I was really excited, then the alarm clock went off and woke me up. I've never been so disappointed in all my life. Sadly, I haven't had a flying dream since, not for want of trying. Perhaps whatever was causing the fear for the original nightmares has gone, and that's what I had as my trigger.

## Out-of-body sensations and illness

Illness is a major trigger of out-of-body sensations, even when the condition is not critical. It's almost as if when the physical body is not working, the spirit body gets in the driving seat. As in the following case, this can bring temporary relief.

Belinda, from London, England, whose ghostly experience at boarding school I describe on pages 36–7, had an out-of-body experience when she was sick.

> I was very ill with asthma as a child. One time I was sitting in my bed and barely able to breathe when I heard my grandma come up the stairs with my dinner. Suddenly, I realised I was up at the ceiling and could breathe quite well. I could see myself still on the bed leaning forward, seemingly in the 'fight for breath' position. Anyhow, as much as I enjoyed being able to breathe easily for a change, I felt I had to get back to my body before my grandma came in with my dinner. The next thing was that I was unable to breathe well again.

Donna, whom I met in central Sweden, described how she suffered from mobility difficulties as a child, owing to a problem at birth, and spent hours sitting in a chair on the verandah of the family's remote, red, wooden house in the forest. She told me that from about the age of three she would have the amazing sensation that her legs were running fast and she could feel them brushing against foliage. During these experiences, which lasted up to ten minutes but seemed much longer, she could go out of the garden, through the pine woods and roam all over the nearby lakeside area. When her mother called out to her, there would be an inrush of air and a bumping sensation, as if someone had knocked into her chair. After an out-of-body experience, Donna found that for several hours her mobility would improve. Donna's mother called these incidents her 'sleeps with her eyes open'.

When Donna became a teenager, the family obtained a car, and she saw some of the places she had 'seen' and described in vivid detail in her childhood.

Donna's experiences are akin to the remote viewing ones experienced by Alison (see page 107). However, in Donna's case, she was aware of actual movement and of wind.

When Connie, from Yorkshire, England, was a teenager, she was very ill in hospital with meningitis.

> After my parents had visited me, they went home and went to bed. My mother said to my father that I was in bed with them. Then my father could also feel my presence. The following evening when they visited me, I told them I had slept with them that night. From that day I started to recover.

Though Connie's parents did not actually see her, they felt her presence. Did both parents and child tune in to each other at a time of distress? Bedtime when a child is absent can be particularly poignant for the parents, and Connie was probably thinking of home and family. Or did Connie 'travel' home for comfort? The experience, or her belief in it, may have triggered some psychological strength in Connie that gave her immune system a kick.

Connie's experience may be an example of the spirit double or doppelganger phenomenon that I mentioned on page 104.

## Near-death experiences

Dr Melvin Morse, a significant researcher into near-death experiences, has estimated that about 70 per cent of children who die momentarily in an accident, operation or serious illness have a near-death experience. Near-death experiences for adults and children include some of the following:

※ A sense that the self has moved beyond the body, usually by floating. The person looks down on their own inert body.

※ Travelling through a dark space or tunnel towards a point of light, sometimes accompanied by rushing wind. This can occasionally be frightening, especially if the journey seems to be downwards.

※ Reaching a place filled with golden or white light, usually resulting in a sensation of bliss. There may be beautiful gardens or clouds.

※ Meeting deceased relatives recognised from life or verified as relatives after the experience by old photographs. Children sometimes see living relatives who call them back to life.

※ Encounters with sacred beings of light, angels or other beings from one's own or other religious traditions. Alternatively, an authoritative voice may be heard.

Near-death accounts from children are especially valuable as evidence of the phenomenon, since children know nothing of the common characteristics of the near-death experience and so their reports are totally free of preconceptions. On the whole, however, few adults who have experienced them when younger are willing to talk except anonymously. This is understandable, as such experiences generally trigger intense personal life change and are often associated with a traumatic event sooner forgotten. I discovered fascinating accounts of adult and childhood near-death experiences in the files of the International Association for Near Death Studies and have collected a number of my own from around the world.

Children's reports of near-death experiences tend to be less elaborate than adults', but they have an especially vivid pictorial quality. Even for a young child such experiences are filled with emotion, and a child or teenager may need years of support to be able to use them positively and not suffer trauma as a result.

### The near-death experiences of very young children

Often the experiences of very young children consist of one or two vivid pictures, which may stay with the child all their life – often with the result that they lose any fear of dying.

Pauline, from Wiltshire, England, was not much more than two when she had her near-death experience.

> I was given up by the doctors when I almost died of pneumonia. I seemed to pass through a dark tunnel, not very pleasant, then skipped along on bright green grass holding someone's hand. I did not know who it was, only that I was very, very happy, and I think it was a man. I remember the hand and half the arm, but what sticks in my mind is the green grass.

The simplest stories involve the child floating above their body. Mike, from the West Midlands, in England, was nearly five when he had this experience.

> It was Christmas. I remember it as if it was yesterday. I was very excited that Christmas was almost upon us, in spite of the war. I remember rushing out to buy my dad cigarettes in the freezing weather without a coat before my mother could stop me. Anyway, the next thing I recall is that I was extremely ill, so much so that my mother set up a bed for me in the front room next to the fire. After that I don't remember much except for one vivid memory.
>
> Suddenly, I was in a position near the door, looking across at the corner where my bed was. Everything, including my mind, was crystal-clear. I could see myself lying on the bed, blond-haired and angel-faced, with my eyes closed. I remember being fascinated at the sight of my nostrils pumping in and out as I laboured to breathe, and I remember thinking, 'Wow, I do look sick!'
>
> Being over the door at this point and being so young, I assumed that everybody could see themselves without having to be in their bodies. This was my last thought before I was aware of a cold stethoscope being pressed to my chest and seeing our old family doctor looking at me and saying to my mother, 'You almost lost him. He's got pneumonia and only pulled through with your care.'

Oona, who lives in Ireland, also had very bad pneumonia, when she was about seven.

I can recall being in my parents' bed, in my parents' bedroom, with a fire in the grate. I was very hot, in pain and distressed. The next second I was high above, looking down, and all the pain was gone. I floated above the bed and looked at myself and my parents. I felt a bit sad for them but happy for myself that I could leave my body behind. As I turned to the top corner of the room, out of the golden haze my mother's voice said, 'Oona, oh, Oona,' and the next minute I was back in my bed with all the pain.

Afterwards I looked back on the experience with some surprise but dared not relate it to anyone for fear of ridicule. But it was so real to me, and still is, that I have never feared death since. If this life was all we had, then it would be illogical and rather a poor deal for some.

Marie, from Lancashire, England, also had a very simple experience as a child of three or four.

There was a flooded mine close to our house, and while I was playing there, I slipped and was washed away. I scrabbled frantically and was rescued by workmen nearby. I put up a plucky fight but, unfortunately, got some water in my lungs. I became very ill and was at death's door. I remember clearly in the middle of the night my father looking down on me. I said, 'I have just been flying very fast through a tunnel with a light at the end.' He told me I had been seeing my own bedside light, which was a small paraffin lamp (we had no electricity). I loved my dad and accepted his explanation and never spoke of it again.

Childhood memories of near-death experiences usually retain their grip through life. Lily, who is 80 years old and lives in Wales, still recalls a detailed experience.

When I was seven, I had measles and was very ill. How long I lay in bed I don't know, but I was in a lane where there were very high ornamental gold gates. Inside was the most beautiful garden – no lawn, path or anything, but flowers of every kind. Those that attracted me most were the madonna lilies, delphiniums and roses, but there were many, many more. I thought how I would love to go in.

I pushed the gates and they gave way, but try as I might I could not get in. There was something behind me or on both sides that seemed to be stopping me. I was so upset, but in the end I gave up trying. I opened my eyes and saw my mother and father crying. My mother looked at me and almost shouted, 'Look, Dad.' I never told anyone, but I can remember it as if it was yesterday.

Frances, from London, England remembered this experience from 1914 or 1915.

> When I was four or five years old, I was very ill. At the same time my father was very ill in another room with double pneumonia and pleurisy. There was a nurse looking after us both, and my mother was dividing her time between my father and me. At that time I was an only child.
>
> Quite suddenly, I became aware of a shiny white person (my description afterwards to my mother) standing at the foot of my bed. I still remember this quite clearly. He was radiating light and he had no wings. He asked if I would like to go away with him, and I saw a lovely place with green grass and sunshine and children playing. It was clear to me that I had a choice, and I felt a longing to go, but then I thought that my mother would not be able to manage without me and so refused.

## Near-death experiences in older children and teenagers

Rob saw his mother trying to pull him back into life as he was dying. He was nine. An appendectomy had left part of the appendix still inside him, and it became septic.

> By the time of my second operation, my condition was serious, and at one point clinical death occurred. I can only recall two images: the first was looking down on my body on the operating table and being turned over by green-clad surgeons and nurses. This image is particularly vivid and, despite its goriness, was not associated with any pain or distress.
>
> The second image is of a blackness with a pinpoint of light far off in the distance. I felt drawn to the light, but there was a feeling that I did not want to pull towards it. My mother is with me in this scene, trying to pull me back from the light. There is also a wind rushing past towards the light. Again, this image is startlingly clear, unlike many other things I remember from that time. I remember little else except coming round after the operation in total panic, made worse by the fact that I couldn't move – due to the after-effects of the anaesthetic I assume.

Kathleen who lives in Vancouver, Canada, sent me this account of her near-death experience at the age of 14.

> My near-death/out-of-body experience happened when my family was on a notorious stretch of highway en route to a ski holiday in the interior. My sister was driving when the road conditions deteriorated. Curiously, my father and I had not been wearing our seatbelts, and I pointed this out to him only moments before the accident. We fastened them. Then we hit black ice, and my sister lost control of the – fortunately heavy – station wagon.

We didn't flip. We crashed through the roadside barrier and flew off a cliff. I experienced this from two perspectives at the same time. In the car I experienced the moment we went off the road until we crashed into a boulder far below like a black-and-white film viewed frame by frame. At the same time I was outside and I watched the airborne car fly over me in slow motion, but in colours. My first thought upon coming to, my head on the dashboard, was, 'How are we going to get the car back on the road?'

We were very lucky that no one was killed or permanently injured.

Phoebe had a very bad attack of scarlet fever when she was 17, before the Second World War. In the old fever hospital, where nuns cared for her, she was not expected to last the night. Later in life, she told her daughter that she remembered looking down on her body lying on the bed with the nuns and the doctor standing next to it. She remembers feeling very much at peace and floating down a spiral. She could hear soothing music, but it was not being played on any specific instrument. She was going down the spiral into something clean, white and cotton-woolly, beckoned by a shadow. It did not have a face but was a nice shape.

Suddenly, Phoebe felt something cold pressed on her forehead and was back on the bed. A nun had put a cold sponge on her head. Without this intervention, Phoebe would have gone on down the spiral.

Phoebe's daughter, Jan, did not know about her mother's experience until she was 15 and angry that her grandfather had died. Jan asked her mother what the point of living was if it always ended in death. Phoebe told her this story and said that since then she had not been afraid of dying.

## Negative reactions to near-death encounters

In some cases, a childhood near-death experience colours a person's attitude to life negatively. They may feel that they should have died and even, in extreme cases, attempt suicide.

Even if the encounter is beautiful, a glimpse of the afterlife can occasionally make the experiencer unsettled in their daily life. Josie, from Northumberland, England, had her near-death experience while suffering from peritonitis as a young teenager. She says:

I seemed to float along an empty corridor towards, and then into, a brilliant light with indefinable shades of pastel-like colours. There was what I can only describe as billions of beautiful shimmering forms – no outlines, as they were all cloaked in whitish garments of translucent light. I longed to be able to tell my parents not to grieve. If only they knew how joyously happy I was, they would rejoice instead.

I often wish I had not been brought back. Then I would not have had to live through the many problems that have beset my life and I would have died in total peace. Death can come at any time, and I have no fear of it.

Josephine has spent her life trying to re-create a near-death experience that occurred during an operation at the age of 12 in France.

Everything went too fast for me. One minute I was in a deep, dark sleep and then suddenly I was in a place with mid-pinkish clouds everywhere, hazy, soft, pinkish, light, very comforting. Next I was wandering through rooms. There was beautiful music. It was so smooth, soft and harmonious. I was so much at ease and felt so relieved and peaceful. I floated through these rooms at a higher level than I walked at that age. In fact, I nearly grazed the ceiling. It seemed to me that we were looking for something. Some quiet presence was with me.

Then we were in a room, and there below me the doctors, masked and gowned, bent over what was me. 'More glucose,' one was saying. Then I had a shock. It seemed like they were talking right next to me, yet I was looking at them from above.

'Which do you wish?' insisted the presence. 'You don't have to go back. The choice is up to you.' There was no pressure to choose, but I thought about Mum and Dad. In a flash, I was back in the operating theatre. A voice said firmly, 'She is waking.'

I must have been given some more anaesthetic, because all I can remember is grasping someone's hand hard and drifting back into normal sleep. For me, there was no whoosh or warning that I was about to return. It was a great shock that happened at the moment I thought about my loved ones. The experience made me feel very strange. I spoke to no one about it. I became either very enthusiastic about things or depressed as I remembered how happy I had been in that state. I am now 22 and at last have learned to control my desire to return.

I once worked at a fun fair when we lived in the United States, taking rides in a desperate attempt to create the feeling of flying. I cut my hair and had it dyed red and took delight in anything pink and puffy. While I lived with my parents, I could control my desire to return to that other place, but the moment I came back to England to university, it was all set free.

Sometimes I seemed to be controlled by something that was not me, and I wondered if I had brought something back with me. I have so regretted this choice I had but did not take, though there are times I am proud of my choice.

There is so much controversy over whether near-death experiences are scientifically verifiable that those who have them sometimes get forgotten by science and are left to struggle with the burden of their experience.

### More unusual near-death experiences

Not all children who have a near-death experience are dying; indeed, it seems that the spiritual sensitivity of children opens them to glimpses of another world as a result of surgical intervention. The fact that children in accidents, who have not had an anaesthetic, report a similar scenario suggests that it is not a chemical reaction to a drug that causes a brush with the afterlife. Fourteen-year-old Ben's experience is remarkable because he is autistic and communicates through a mixture of speech and sign language. It is unlikely that he would have had any knowledge of near-death experiences.

Ben described an experience of 'being a ghost' during an operation – in the course of which he also met Sai Baba (the family are followers of the Indian holy man). His mother, Jane, from Sussex, England, told me:

> I asked Ben what he meant. He said that when he was asleep during the operation, he was looking down from the ceiling and saw himself lying on the table as the doctors operated on him. He said the doctors were wearing masks and green gowns, and he was lying with his eyes closed.
>
> Ben described going through the wall to a place like a big cloud. There he saw Sai Baba, who welcomed him and materialised 'vibhuti' (sacred healing ash) that he then sprinkled over the site of Ben's operation. Then Ben described his grandmother's dog, which had been put to sleep 18 months previously. Ben said the dog was now 'new' and was jumping up excitedly at Sai Baba.
>
> Ben also saw the taxi lady. She had been the escort for the school taxi and had died very suddenly just before Christmas last year. She hugged him and told him to be a good boy. Then he mentioned another lady with eye glasses who turned out to be his Great-auntie Annie, who had died two years earlier.
>
> Ben saw the doctor tapping him on the arm, telling him to wake up. He went quickly back into his body and woke up. Ben does not usually display any emotions, but as he was telling me about his experience, he kept wiping tears from his eyes.

One of the most remarkable near-death accounts I have come across is Megan's. When she was ten years old, Megan, from the north of England, saw Father Christmas during her operation. The other details are typical of a child's near-death experience.

> I had a big operation on my shoulder for a useless arm damaged at birth. My mother had died giving birth to me. I was told later I nearly died during the operation. I had the last rites of the church, which I do not remember. I had been looking forward to Christmas even though I was in hospital. What I saw was the loveliest bright light. Then I saw Father Christmas going through that lovely ray

of light. I could see him going up and up. Before he got to the top, I heard someone call my name, 'Meg! Meg!' which they used to call me in those days. The bright light seemed to fade away from me. Father Christmas was gone. I felt someone holding my hand, saying, 'Don't die, Meggie.' I opened my eyes to see my father crying and then I began to recover. I will never forget that wonderful light, a light I have never seen again.

The vividness and strange imagery of the near-death experience of six-year-old Jacques were not those of a child's normal visions of angels or God but seem to have come from ancient mythology. This account comes from India many years ago.

When a youth, I had a fall of some considerable height, landing head first on concrete. When I arrived at the hospital, the doctors pronounced me dead and issued a death certificate. My parents were told I must be interred at once because of the heat. They would not agree, and I was placed in a room that was in the main constructed of marble and left there three days.

On the third day, a nurse came in and saw a slight movement and found that I was alive.

All I can recall is that I was walking along a rough-hewn tunnel with walls that looked as if the rocks were of copper and gold, lit by firebrands on the walls. I felt no fear and continued down the tunnel till I came to a round chamber cut in this strange rock of copper and gold, and there seated on a marble seat of very beautiful design was this enormous figure of a man in a white robe with long, flowing white hair and beard. He looked as old as time itself and yet as young as a boy.

I made as if to run towards this force of love, strength, power, light and perfection. Suddenly, a look of foreboding came on his face. He raised his hand and I could go no further. Then, with a lovely smile, that hand gently pushed me back with the words, 'Not now, not now,' echoing in my ears. It was then I shall always believe I came back from the dead.

## When a child has an out-of-body experience

If a small child talks about floating or flying downstairs and is nervous of staircases, especially at night, reassure them that this is a special kind of dream, but emphasise that they must never try to jump downstairs when they are awake, as they may hurt their physical body.

If an older child or teenager reports an out-of-body sensation, explain about beliefs in the spiritual body. Reassure them that there is no way they can get detached from their physical body during sleep. This may be a good opportunity to discuss any worries about death.

If they have flying dreams, especially frightening ones, suggest that while dreaming they try to fly or float where they want. Explain that they are in total control of their dreams all the time. Children and adolescents do not need to be taught lucid dreaming. To be told that they can overcome scary monsters by flying away is usually enough to enable them to do so – and a good antidote to nightmares.

Discourage your adolescent from experimenting with out-of-body experiences or from reading sensationalist magic books, and explain that these are quite normal powers but ones that should be allowed to occur spontaneously and not cultivated. You could compensate by offering the opportunity to fly in a plane (with budget airlines, a short trip abroad can cost very little).

Make sure your older child has plenty of physical adventures related to nature, such as supervised tree- or rock-climbing, rather than simulated theme park rides, which only distort reality.

## When a child has a near-death experience

If your child has an accident or operation, even if it is not life-threatening, allow them to talk about their feelings and experiences afterwards. Some may well be the effects of anaesthetic but are no less important for that. Sometimes in all the concern about physical recovery, the emotional aspects can be sidelined unintentionally.

Hospitals can bring all kinds of questions into a child's mind about illness, disability and death, so use the opportunity to discuss these matters. You don't have to give your child beliefs that are alien to your own, but you can explain theories of the afterlife.

If your child attends a church, synagogue, mosque or religious school, they may have encountered ideas of hell. Even some adults have lingering fears of a system of retribution that was created by the Church Fathers many centuries ago to keep the faithful in line. Reassure your child that a loving deity or benign force is not any different from a loving parent, and so nothing nasty will happen after death. You can use the opportunity to discuss the whole concept of wrongdoing and putting right wrongs. The Buddhist and Hindu system of karma is no bad starting point.

Should your child have a full near-death experience (rare, since serious accidents and illnesses in childhood are mercifully uncommon), ask them if they had any unusual dreams while they were asleep or unconscious. Drawing these out may take time and patience. Don't be surprised if your child is very upset or, on the other hand, very excited about what they saw. Allow them to talk over and over again about their feelings, but include plenty of earthly input – jokes, games, hugs and cuddles, etc. – to ease the child back into everyday childhood life.

Usually, a loving parent is more effective than even the most highly trained expert in helping a child or teenager to adjust, but – fortunately – the medical profession is now beginning to take near-death experiences more seriously.

# CHAPTER 8

# Children and Past Lives

Reincarnation, the belief that our soul returns to a new body after death, is accepted by about two-thirds of the world's population, mainly in the East, and is thousands of years old. Such philosophies regard progressive lives as lessons that need to be learned or as a means of righting omissions in past lives. Since the 1960s, belief in reincarnation has grown in the Western world with the increasing popularity of the search for enlightenment through Eastern spirituality.

But even if individual past lives seem improbable, we know that all human life came out of East Africa several million years ago. Therefore all of us share the same genetic heritage. It may be that it is possible for a young child to dip into the well of this collective past experience, called by the psychotherapist Jung 'the collective unconscious'. From this well we can draw up memories of lives that bear similarities with our own or, more personally, of ancestors known or unknown.

### Evidence for reincarnation among children

Dr Ian Stevenson is Head of the Department of Psychiatric Medicine at the University of Virginia and has studied reincarnation for more than 30 years. Dr Stevenson found that young children gave the most consistent results in past-life recollection but that they lost spontaneous recall of earlier worlds at about the age of seven.

Perhaps the most significant evidence for reincarnation in Stevenson's research is his finding that 35 per cent of 895 children who claimed to remember previous lives possessed either birthmarks of an unusual kind or had birth defects not linked to any apparent genetic or physiological cause. These birth scars correlated with wounds apparently inflicted on the person whose life the child recalled as his or her own in an earlier existence. What is more, medical corroboration, usually in the form of a post-mortem report, was obtained in a significant number of these cases. For example, a Burmese child claimed she was the reincarnation of her aunt, who had died during surgery for congenital heart disease. The child was born with a long, vertical linear birthmark in the same place as her late aunt's surgical incision.

Although children who remember previous lives come from many cultures, the majority of the cases in Stevenson's research were reported in southern Asia, possibly because parents in this area are more willing to take their children's reports of past lives seriously. In the UK especially, a child who talks of a past life at school is likely to be referred to a psychiatrist, such claims being viewed – quite wrongly – as symptomatic of family trauma.

Many parents of children who report past lives are understandably unwilling to allow their children to be investigated by researchers. From my own research, I know that generally the most dramatic cases are rarely spoken of outside the home. If they are told to me, it is in confidence, because I am a mother too.

## The case of Shanti Devi

The case of Shanti Devi is probably the most famous of all documented instances of childhood past-life memories and dates back to the 1930s. A committee of prominent men appointed by Mahatma Gandhi investigated the case. They took Shanti from her home near Delhi to the village where she claimed to have lived in her previous incarnation as Lugdi, wife of Kedarnath Chaube.

From the age of four, Shanti had talked about her husband in Mathura, who, she said, owned a cloth shop. She called herself Chaubine (Chaube's wife). When she was eight, she reluctantly gave her former husband's full name. She described her husband in detail and also mentioned that her husband's shop was located in front of Dwarkadhish temple. This was discovered on her later visit to be the exact location, but, as she predicted, the shop was closed at that time of day.

When Shanti was six years old, she gave an account of her death following childbirth, including details of the complicated surgical procedures that were used in attempts to save her. As she grew older, she became desperate to be taken to Mathura, and at last a relative of Kedarnath was sent to visit her. Shanti recognised her husband's cousin, instantly described her former home and mentioned a place where she had hidden some money before her death. At last her former husband came to Delhi, but to mislead Shanti he was introduced to her as his elder brother. Shanti identified him correctly, and her earlier description matched precisely, including a wart on the left side of his cheek, near his ear. Shanti also described a well in the courtyard of the house at Mathura, where she used to take her bath. This was hidden by a stone when Shanti visited her former home, accompanied by the Committee members, but she nevertheless identified the exact spot.

On the journey from the station, Shanti guided the driver to her former home, pointing out changes made to the area since her death. On the journey she insisted on stopping to greet an elderly person in the crowd, whom she correctly identified as her former father-in-law. At the house

Shanti took the Committee to the second floor to show them the hiding place for her money. No money was found, but her husband later admitted he had removed the money after his wife's death.

## Glimpses of the past

For every case that is verifiable by ongoing or retrospective investigation, a thousand more exist in which the child refers to the past life only once. Psychic researcher Joe Cooper told me of an 18-month-old child who, when seated on a motor bike by an adult, suddenly announced, 'I was killed on a motor bike when I was 17.' At the time the infant could hardly say more than single words and could never be persuaded to repeat the words again.

It can be frustrating for parents and researchers when a child makes an amazing statement about something they could not have known about and then refuses to say any more. But these brief insights should be valued and accepted all the same. Were these children making up a story, it would be rich in detail, with a beginning, a middle and an end. Once we start testing or questioning their experience, the child may feel pressurised to invent details or may simply clam up.

William who lives in Southampton, England, told me:

> When my wife's nephew, Alan, was of pre-school age, he would sometimes talk about his other mummy. He said that it was much better living in his present home because he was no longer cold and hungry. Alan's parents were very religious and shied away from such talk. They sought some advice and were told to ignore it. China seems to have been involved, but the details were so few.

Jilly, who lives in Lancashire, England, said:

> My husband, Martin, and I had just redecorated the study and bought a new lamp for the desk. It looked like an old-fashioned gas lamp, and as soon as my son Adrian saw it, he pointed and said, 'Gas.'
>
> He was just two and had a fairly basic limited vocabulary and hadn't even been with us when we bought it. Martin and I hadn't said anything, and of course Adrian had never seen a gas lamp before.

In many past-life accounts the child suddenly develops a wider vocabulary, but only in connection with the past life. Jean's daughter, Bryony, from Berkshire, England, was three and also did not talk very much. Then she suddenly said, 'Mummy, why don't I have brown hair?' Her mother explained that all the family had fair hair and showed her family photos. But Bryony persisted. Finally, Jean ran out of patience and said, 'Because you haven't.'

'But I did have brown hair,' Bryony explained, 'before I was a baby, when I used to look after the sick people in the Church.'

Bryony never mentioned the subject again. As I have said, these fleeting memories don't come complete with name, date and library references, but seem like a sudden glimpse that fades as instantly as it came.

Children can have a less tangible sense of having lived before, and this can be quite unsettling. Another Jean, who comes from Essex, England, wrote to me through my website.

> I've often wondered if I've lived before. As a child I had scary dreams. My entire body was falling through time and space. When I was 12, I was in school at my desk writing the date and had a weird thought come to me. The date seemed a long, long way into the future, and I suddenly thought, 'The world has changed a lot.' Why did I think that? As I've grown older, I often feel that I'm constantly searching for a particular lifestyle or place.

Children who recall previous lives tend to speak of them almost as soon as they learn to talk, and in some cases may identify a particular place, time and background that they could not have known about from their present-life experience. They may also display detailed knowledge of old-fashioned artefacts or use snatches of a language or dialect alien to their current home culture. These are connected with the past life.

## Recalling other worlds

Bernadette is an international author and environmentalist. She is convinced that her daughter has memories of a previous life and says that the connection between herself and her daughter began at the moment of conception.

> When I conceived my baby, I saw her in the act of love, and when she was born, she was exactly the child I had visualised. While I was pregnant with my daughter, I had a vivid dream that she was standing in front of me, a small baby, the size of a toddler. Yet my daughter did not look as if she was a toddler, although she could speak. She told me her name, and I responded, 'Don't you think we should wait?'
>
> 'Oh, no,' she replied, 'babies choose their own names, and mine is Alexandria.'
>
> I looked the name up in a dictionary and, of course, realised that Alexandria was a place in Egypt.
>
> When she was still tiny, Alex saw a picture of an angel. 'That's a glory angel,' she told me. 'They sing to you when you are a baby.'
>
> From when Alex was tiny she loved painting, using brilliant colours, and her pictures showed remarkable expertise in dimension and perspective for one so young. One day, when she

was about two-and-a-half, Alex was painting in the kitchen, and I remarked, 'You are very good at painting. Would you like to be a painter when you grow up?'

'Oh, no,' she replied. 'I've been that already. I had to paint the King and Queen at the court.'

I tried to coax Alex to repeat her remark, but she never said it again. At about the same age, it was a hot day and Alex was sitting with her legs crossed, totally relaxed. 'It was like this on the beach in Brazil,' she told me.

I had never been to Brazil and certainly never mentioned the place. However, two years before I conceived Alexandria, a clairvoyant told me that I would have a daughter who had been a Brazilian princess. She had chosen to come back because she had great psychic abilities but been spoiled and wasted her life in Brazil, so wanted to get it right with me.

Alex has continued to paint. One day she cried out in frustration, 'I just cannot remember how to draw a chameleon.'

When Alex was only two, I took her to the National Gallery, in London. A friend who came along warned me that Alex would be bored within five minutes but was astounded, as we were there for more than four hours. Alex was totally absorbed the whole time. She was especially fascinated by the paintings by Picasso and Monet. There was a lady painting a picture of a Monet, and Alex sat down and drew the woman painting. It had all the right dimensions.

Alex and I are very close. If she is with my mother, I will ring and know that she has asked to come home. My mother and I always phone at the same time too. Alexandria did once tell me her Brazilian name. I wrote it down on a piece of paper but frustratingly have never been able to find it.

## Trauma and past lives

An operation can trigger past-life recall in young children. Jared comes from Essex, England. He was two and was only just talking when he had a major operation on his head to fuse the bones around his fontanel. He needed three major blood transfusions. Some spiritual researchers consider that the fontanel is where the soul enters the infant's body before birth and that this is the reason the baby's fontanel is still soft at birth.

Jared's father, Ron, told me:

Two or three weeks after the operation, Jared started to talk about a Victorian house and how he was dressed in thin, what seemed to be ragged, clothes. The house, he said, was cold and damp and in a city, and he ate mainly bread and water. The food was boring.

The details were so vivid that it sounded to his parents like a scene from the 1850s. Jared talked about the Victorian world for about three or four months to his mother, father and grandmother as though he had lived there. Jared is now nine years old. The details have faded, and he doesn't really want to talk about it now.

Could it be that for Jared the operation triggered some unidentified part of the brain where past-life recall resides? As in a number of other accounts, he was able to use complex language and display unusual knowledge, but only in relation to the past world.

## Past lives and psychometry

Sometimes what looks like past-life recall can actually be a case of psychometry – another psychic phenomenon in which contact with a place or an object triggers knowledge about a person or people connected with it. (This was the case in Linda's experience in Florida, which I recounted on page 49.) A sensitive child may pick up information about a tragic event that has become imprinted on the thing or place and may relive some of the sensations involved. I suspect this is what happened in the following case of Alison, from North Carolina, USA.

> We were travelling through British Columbia, in Canada, in the spring. We stopped at a hotel where the proprietor had put together a ghost town from a collection of buildings brought from elsewhere. Included was a wonderfully restored saloon, which we visited. The rest of the family had gone down the steps and were walking along the road when there was an agonised cry from Timothy, my four-year-old son, who was stumbling down the steps. Clutching his head, he was screaming that someone was trying to break his head. He described the pain as like a knife. I immediately thought of brain tumours, but neither before or since has he ever complained of pain. The situation we were in and the terror it provoked for those few minutes in fact convinced me that he was involved in an experience from the past.

## Past-life dreams

Many children and teenagers dream of past lives. They usually describe these experiences as something more than ordinary dreams. They are highly coloured and detailed, and the emotions tend to be very strong. Like other psychic dreams, the past-life dream remains in the memory far longer than the usual kind of dream, which is tidied up by the conscious mind relatively quickly. The child may be reluctant to leave the dream and become frustrated that they cannot return the following night.

A few months ago, my own son Bill had a dream that was more than just a dream. At the time of writing it is still so vivid that he is writing a story about it, as he says it feels like part of his life. In the dream Bill was tall, broad and dark (in real life he is tall and well-built but very fair). He was in a place that was probably Sicily or another part of Italy, where the people were olive-skinned. He was aware that they were speaking a different language, although he could understand them.

Bill worked for an older, short Mob boss with grey hair. He was in love with the boss's daughter, and they decided to run away together. They were on the dock going towards a ferry when he was surrounded by the boss and his men, who shot him in the chest. Bill was aware that he had died.

When Bill told me about the dream, he was very angry and said he felt cheated. I would have dismissed the dream as just that except that Bill has a huge red keloid scar in the centre of his chest, right where he said he was shot. The scar was very tiny at birth but has grown larger throughout his life. What is more, Bill's taste in fantasy is *Buffy the Vampire Slayer* or *Alien Encounters*. He does not like Mafia films and usually walks out if one is showing – unusual for someone who devours gory films

Debbie, whose flying dream is described on page 111, also recalls a teenage past-life dream.

> I dreamt I was inside a shed of some sort as a prisoner. There was a window, and outside I could see a soldier marching up and down with a gun over his shoulder. It was quite dark in this shed but light outside, so the soldier was silhouetted. I don't know if there were others in there with me, but I think so. Then the soldier turned and faced the window, aimed his gun and fired many times through the walls. I was hit and died. I lay there in darkness. I realised that now nothing could keep me imprisoned and was very aware that I was a ghost.
>
> I wafted outside, saw a huge building where I seemed to know there were many people imprisoned and had a strong desire to free them, so floated into the building and opened all the doors and told everyone to get out.
>
> I have never forgotten this dream. As a child I hated any form of war film. I would never watch them. This dream was not triggered by anything I'd read or seen on TV as far as I know.

## Wartime experiences

Wartime past lives are probably among the most common, perhaps because so many people die traumatically in war. The cutting short of a past life must surely be a powerful incentive to recall that life and try to resolve fears it may have triggered.

Pam, who lives in County Durham, England, wrote to me describing her young son's spontaneous past-life recall.

> We were travelling to Sunderland one day in June 1996. We were just coming into a small village on the outskirts of Sunderland when our son Adam, who was in the back seat of the car, pointed

to a spot just in front of a bridge we were about to go under, saying he had died over there.

A bit further along the road, Adam pointed to the same spot from a different direction and repeated that he had been killed at the place. As Adam was only three-and-a-half, it was a shock for us. I asked how he had died. Adam told me that he had been in a plane and that it had crashed. He kept saying that it was not an accident but that he had died on purpose. We let the matter rest for a couple of weeks.

When we questioned Adam again, he told us about the plane, which was a quiet one, not a fast one like a jet, flying round and round.

I wanted to find out more. I telephoned the Sunderland Air Museum and asked them about the crash. The curator told me that it was a British plane during the Second World War, and the only person who had been killed was the pilot. A book had been written about him, as he was a hero, because he had lost his own life avoiding crashing on the town. I managed to get hold of the book. As I read it, so many of the things confirmed the details Adam was gradually revealing.

About a month before Christmas, Adam suddenly took the book from my desk and said that the photo of the man on the front was him before he died. Though many of the pilot's friends and family were pictured, Adam always pointed out the pilot among them, even at different ages, and insisted that it was himself.

Paul, from Chester, England, wrote to me through my website.

My problems are I am now a teenager. I am lost in total confusion about my life. I am disabled and spiritual. I am not at school because I upset my peers and some of my teachers, and I also have problems at home.

I started to recall past lives when my great-grandma died seven years ago. My first recall was World War Two. I was an agent called Bertie, aged 30, and working for the British. I was caught behind enemy lines and I was tortured by my own parents. I do not know if I died at the hands of them, but they were SS.

I do not mean to do nasty things, but I can't forgive them. And I do not know how to stop the pain and the hurt I feel. I also miss my great-grandma because she was my true mother in the past life. Please can you try to help me understand why this is happening.

For Paul, past-life recall is heightened by present-day trauma, and he needs earthly support. Regardless of the authenticity of his past life, which was certainly was very vivid, he is feeling alienated from everyone in the present. In the same way, he believes that family members betrayed him in his past life because he was fighting on the wrong side. Paul also had a First World War memory in which his family again betrayed him. It was his mother, who is also struggling, who initially wrote to me about Paul's experiences.

Ideally, children and teenagers would be able to talk to professionals about their past lives, and those professionals would then be able to use the information for practical positive intervention where there is present trauma. It is my belief, however, that professionals dealing with young people currently lack the necessary training in how to help with traumatic occult experiences. Until they get this training, many young people will continue to write to researchers like myself. I hope my well-intended practical suggestions were of some use.

## Explaining fears in terms of past lives

In my work with adults, I have found that many phobias, such as claustrophobia and fear of water, can be explained and often resolved in terms of past-life events.

Kathleen, whose teenage near-death experience in a car accident is described on page 117, recounts this strange experience, in which her young son Steve appeared to speak in Spanish although the whole family is Canadian.

> My son was about one at the time, and his vocabulary consisted of 'mama' and occasionally perhaps 'papa'. Steve was in a back carrier, and we went for a walk in the forest. It had been raining heavily, and when we came to the road, the culverts were gushing with water coming down the mountain. My son became very excited, and he pointed to the rushing water and said, 'Agua! Agua, agua, agua!'
>
> Needless to say, I thought this was extremely bizarre, as he had never been exposed to any Spanish, nor heard any other word for water but 'water'.
>
> His behaviour around water in the years that followed had us wondering if he was once a Spanish speaker who had died by drowning in a previous life. Although he was an extremely good-natured and happy toddler, bathtime was a nightmare. We couldn't go anywhere near a beach. I couldn't go swimming in his view because he absolutely freaked out, acting as though I would be swallowed up and lost forever. Seeing other people in the water did not bother him. It took years and years before he finally learned how to swim. And when I forced him to go on my father's sailboat for a weekend, he went into a white-knuckled state of shock when we had a good wind. Now he refuses to go.

Four-year-old Connor, who lives in Australia, has had a number of psychic experiences. As in Connor's case, young children who have past-life recall often go on to experience other psychic phenomena. Connor's mother, Richeena, told me:

While in the bath while quite small, Connor was pushing one of his toys under the water. He said it had died, and then he told me quite matter-of-factly that when you die, you are born again to Mummy and Daddy. My grandmother's twin sister drowned in a boating accident about 80 years ago.

Then Connor and I had similar dreams on the same night. He said he was drowning and he saw an octopus under the water. I dreamed he was drowning and I couldn't save him. I went under the water but I could not reach him. A few weeks later it really happened, not with Connor but with his younger brother, Hunter. We were at the swimming pool, and Hunter went under the water, and I couldn't get him, and he almost drowned. His cousin pulled him out.

I have a daughter and granddaughter in New Zealand. One day Connor rang his niece, Claudia. Claudia is 20 months older than Connor. I was asleep. New Zealand is two hours ahead of us. I had no idea he was phoning her. We do not know how he dialled the numbers, as they were not on speed dial or on any paper he could have read, nor were they the last number dialled. We never got billed for the call either. Connor and Claudia are very close, almost like twins. They grew up together until we left New Zealand to come to Australia 18 months ago. They miss each other very much.

## Past lives and regression

Usually I have a strict 'no under-18s policy' for past-life work, even though I use only light relaxation techniques and never hypnosis even with adults. However, 16-year-old Libby is the daughter of a good friend, and I know her well, so I agreed to help her to go back in time in her mind, with a guided fantasy – rather like a waking dream. This was something she wanted to do, and I didn't want her experimenting with friends. She is also remarkably stable and mature for her age.

Libby's mother, a senior childcare professional, was present, and I explained that if Libby felt at all uncomfortable, we would stop. I also explained that the images would be coming from her mind and not from any external forces and were only images. This is Libby's own account of the experience, which she described as freaky but very cool. Her written account agrees entirely with the actual experience, which occurred some months earlier.

I followed a butterfly through a garden and down ten steps. I was in a boat with no oars and went along a river. At the end of the river I got out and I was standing by a well.

I looked down at my feet and I was wearing brown sandals. I was wearing a white, short type of dress that had short sleeves and was made simply. I was in a small village with white square houses. I went into a house and inside was a square table and some wooden chairs. I knew it was not my house and I went back out again.

I turned around and saw an older girl who was wearing a long white dress with long sleeves, and she was carrying a basket with food in it. She had brown frizzy hair tied in a bun. My hair was almost exactly the same. I felt she was my sister and so I went over to talk to her, and she said she was going to see our uncle, who was ill. She didn't tell me her name, and I didn't know mine either. I was 20 and my sister was 30.

She said our uncle had a bad back and so could not work or look after his family very well. I went with her to my uncle's house and we walked through dirt streets to where it was. When we got there, we went inside. There didn't seem to be any doors on the houses. There was an oldish man, and he was putting things on to a square wooden table. The house looked the same as the first one I had been in. My uncle was about to have dinner and that is why he needed the food.

In the corner of the room were three children, two boys and a girl. One boy was about ten, the other about six, and the girl about eight. The older boy was called Tom, and the girl was called Judith. I don't know what the younger boy was called. They were playing with wooden blocks.

To the right of the door was a small room leading off the main room. It was the bedroom where the family slept. But there was another room to the left of the door. I didn't know what it was. My sister told me that my uncle used to work on a farm but he injured his back, so he got fired. He used to work with a young boy, who my sister was going to marry. They were engaged and he still worked on the farm.

My uncle relied on my mother (his sister) to provide him with food until he got better. My uncle's wife was at the church with my mother. I was not told what they were doing. My uncle had a dog. I think it was a beagle. I left the house and went back to the well.

I went forward ten years in my mind and then I looked down at my feet again. I was wearing brown leather-type shoes that had been sewn together very simply and a long, white long-sleeved dress, the type that my sister had been wearing. I looked around me, and the village/town and the once-white houses looked empty. There was an eerie feeling, as if something had happened and everyone had suddenly left. The place seemed deserted.

I was 30 now and I knew I had a house of my own and I knew where to go. When I got there, I went inside. It was nicer than my uncle's house. There was a proper stove with a big cooking pot over the fire. There was a big wooden table in the middle of the room. I could see a back door in front of me, leading to a back garden. I could see the back garden in my mind's eye. I did not need to go out there.

> My children were in the back garden playing. I think there were
> five of them. I knew I was supposed to cook dinner for my children
> and that my husband would be home from work any minute. But I
> did not want to stay there long. I knew my husband would be
> angry, but I really had to leave. I felt scared, and I had the feeling
> he was really nasty to me and hit me. I left quickly and decided to
> go back to the well.

Libby's mother said there had been no domestic violence in the family, so
Libby wasn't reliving any trauma, and wasn't worried after her experience.

A few weeks after the regression, Libby's aunt came to a family party. She
brought some old family photos that Libby had never seen before. In them
Libby recognised the sister, herself and the two boys from the first
regression scene. When Libby went to a museum in Dorchester recently,
she saw her shoes and clothes, which belonged to 1850s farming families.
She had never seen them before and had no particular interest in history.
Was she linking into the life of an ancestor?

Lilian, herself a healer and past-life expert, was regressed as an adult.
The life she experienced was that of a child who died before he grew up and
which she believes explains her own chronic lung problems as a child in this
lifetime. The experience also helped her to come to terms with an old fear
in this life. Lilian told me:

> I found myself climbing what seemed to be rungs up a long black
> shaft. I was holding some rags, and others were tied round my
> waist. I had a canvas bag round my shoulders with cleaning
> brushes. I knew I was a boy cleaning chimneys and I was choking.
> Then I was in a beautiful room. It was a girl's bedroom with pink
> covers and it was very clean. I was very dirty, so I knew I would
> get in trouble for being there. I would make it dirty.
>
> It was bad in the chimney. I wanted to go to the park, where the
> air was fresh, but the likes of me could not go there. People would
> say: 'Oi, you boy!' and chase me away.
>
> I liked it on top of the roof, straddling the pointed bit. I could
> see the tops of the houses and the church steeple and to the left
> something green. I had something to eat, hard bread and a bit of
> cheese. It was black from my pocket, but it tasted good. I would
> have been happy to live and die there on the roof.
>
> I slept in a little room with a wooden door that would not open
> or close properly. There was straw for a bed, and it opened on to
> an alley.
>
> I wore a dirty black hat with a brim. But when I went out before
> sleep I had another, blue-green hat. Then I was by the river with
> huge great stones and an iron ring on the embankment. A nice lady
> with a stall gave me fish. She was a friend of mine. I could charm
> her to give me fish, but everyone else she made pay.

Then I went back to sleep. It wasn't so nice when I saw the person I was working for. He wore two small capes, one to his hips and one to his shoulders. He had a hat with a brim, not a top hat, and nice shiny boots, with a silver cane and a huge knob on the end. He never got dirty, and we had to run behind his cart. He was my master, and I was scared of him.

In the end he killed me because I had TB. He hit me over the head again and again with the knob on top of his cane. Put me out of my misery, he said. 'It is for the best.'

After the regression I could see the man in black and white like an image. I could not let him go. Then the vision disappeared. I knew him and I had been scared of him in this life ... On the way home it hit me. His eyes were those of my ex-husband, Joe. I was always scared of Joe. He was a bully. I remembered the same eyes coming close to me, menacing, filled with fury. But this time I got away and outlived Joe and left my lung problems behind in childhood.

## Another life, another mother

If reincarnation is a possibility, can the child choose the mother they wish to bond with?

Paul lives in Scotland. It may be that he chose his present family because he knew that his mother would be kind to him. When he was about four years old, his mother was washing his face at teatime. He suddenly pulled back and said, 'Don't wash me there. That's where my mummy hit me.'

His mother was about to say, 'Come on now!' because she was busy, and children come out with all kinds of excuses to avoid the ordeal of soap and water. However, she stopped and said: 'Well, tell me about it then.' He said in an abrupt manner, as if she was stupid, 'You know, that's where she hit me, and I fell down the stairs and died. Not you, Mummy, but the mummy I had before. That's why this time I decided to come to a mummy who would love me.'

Paul's mother could never get him to repeat his remarks. He had not previously expressed any objections to his mother rubbing his face and did not afterwards.

Often this kind of remark is one-off, uttered quite casually. If a parent questions the child, they may become defensive or simply have no recollection of what they said.

Occasionally, memories of the other life can persist for months or even years. Jo, who lives in Nottingham, England, accepted her daughter's 'other family' without making undue fuss, and so Hannah was been able to move away from the overlapping world in her own time.

From a very young age, my daughter Hannah could form her own sentences and until she started school, she regularly talked about her other mother and father. She always referred to this couple as Mother and Father, rarely Mum and Dad. Hannah has always called us by our first names, although we never encouraged her to do so, nor discouraged it.

Hannah told me when she was about two-and-a-half that her father had been killed by a gun. I was quite astounded at the time, because she had no interest in guns. She mentioned her other parents in everyday conversation, and it became a normal topic. Hannah has always talked about life and death from a very young age. She often used to say, 'When I was older than you and lived with my other mother and father ...'

Unfortunately, as Hannah grew older and became aware of imaginary play, the two became muddled and her recollections later became make-believe stories, for example, 'My other mother and father would let me have a kitten if I wanted one.'

An amusing instance regarding Hannah's other mother and father occurred when Sharon, the mother of a friend of Hannah's, began helping out in the nursery class once a week. I had only met Sharon a few times, and it was not until I knew her better that she told me she was very confused about our family. Hannah had told her a few times about her other father and that she did not live with him any more, and Andrew was her father now. As you can imagine, Sharon assumed I had had a partner before Andrew and that Andrew was not her real father.

James, from Berkshire, England, had a more distressing experience of past-life recollection. He first talked of his other family when he was three years old, and became upset when he was unable to find them in this life. His mother Carolyn said:

James is our natural child and has never lived anywhere else but our home.

It all started gradually. James would talk about his other family, but he was obviously anxious not to upset us. He said he had lived with another family before and he did want to be with us, but he would like to go and see them. At first we treated it very light-heartedly and humoured him.

James talked about another father and mother and a sister, which was also strange because his own sister Sarah had not been born then. He also talked about a vehicle they used to have, which appeared to be horse-drawn.

There wasn't anything we could do, because we didn't know where to take him to see this family, but it was awful, because he was at one stage getting very distressed about not seeing them. He would say, 'You know, when I lived in the white house ...' and became more and more anxious and started to cry, begging us to take him to the white house. 'All right, I'll take you,' I promised, but of course I had no idea where it was. There were tears on several occasions. 'I want to go now. Please take me,' he used to say. It was so frustrating. We didn't know where to take him. 'You know, you know,' he would cry. Then it stopped.

A year later James started talking about another life that he went to at night. I have described this on page 101. James was totally happy and settled at home – as he was later at school – so there is no obvious psychological explanation for other lives.

## Coming back to the same family

There is a belief among many reincarnationists that people tend to return to the same group of souls throughout their evolution, albeit in different relationships. The strangest and most intriguing phenomenon is that of grandmothers and great-grandmothers who apparently return as their own granddaughter. This following is one example. Beth, who lives in South Africa, described her daughter Victoria's otherworldly links.

From a very young age Victoria was a strangely compassionate child who talked about concepts like guilt and blame even before she was at nursery school. I was studying for my finals in social work when I was pregnant with her. Even more strangely, Victoria seemed at times to be someone else.

Victoria would use words and make comments which just did not tie in with the fact that she was a child born in 1985. She would look lovingly at me and murmur, 'You were a beautiful baby.' When we drove past the house where I used to live when I was a teenager, she commented, 'I was so happy in that house. I loved living there.'

Victoria talked about speaking another language when she was a child and not having had motor cars then. My 'owma' (Afrikaans for 'granny'), my paternal grandmother, had lived with my parents until her death in 1975. She had always worn her hair long and caught up in a bun. A few years ago, the first time Victoria put up her hair for ballet, I asked her, 'Do you know how?' Victoria called back, 'Don't worry. I've done this billions of times.'

I began wondering whether she might be the reincarnation of my beloved owma, who was the only adult I ever loved. I was very close to my owma, who lived with us, because she only had one son, who was my father, and no daughters at all. She always doted on me, whereas being the eldest in a very 'boys are best' family, I always felt that my parents would have preferred me to be a boy. In fact my first word was 'Mama' addressed to Owma.

Owma almost certainly spoke Hooghallands and drove in horse-drawn carriages as a child, and for as long as I knew her wore her long hair in a bun, expertly pinned on her head. In spite of having no previous interest in reincarnation, I began thinking that Victoria and I had known each other before.

Victoria's paintings and drawings done at playschool almost always included a wispy, fey little waif in the background. When questioned, she shyly admitted, 'That's Ella May, my sister.'

I said, 'But you've never seen her.' Ella May died before Victoria was born.

'Oh yes, I have. I saw her before I was born.'

In other accounts, the child claims to have been a previous sibling who died. Lorna, from London, England, writes:

My daughter's baby was born on Christmas Eve. She was the first girl in the family. When she was six months old, she died. I kept saying, 'She will come back.' Two years later, my daughter had another little girl Suzy, with blue eyes just like the first.

When Suzy was two years old, she accidentally found some photos of the baby's grave covered with flowers. She picked the photos up, ran to her mother and said, 'My flowers, Mummy. Mine, mine.'

'No,' said her mother.

But she kept insisting they were hers. 'Dark, dark trees. Me frightened. Me go way. But me come back. Me not go away again.'

There was a row of tall trees near the baby's grave.

## When a child has a past-life experience

The simple fact is that we do not know whether past lives are actual, ancestral memories transmitted through our genes or a less direct connection with past worlds. However, the experience for the child is real, even if not verifiable, and so should be accepted like any other information. Listen carefully, especially to more detailed recall through dreams, as this can reveal a great deal about a child or teenager's current fears and feelings, whether or not the past life is authentic.

If a child talks of a particular period or place, take them to a museum where objects can be handled and ask them what they feel when they hold different items. Wait and see if they identify certain ones.

Generally, if a child thinks you are questioning them, they will clam up, so instead try asking the child to draw or tell a story about what they have said. Encourage your child to collect pictures and information about the period or place in which their past life took place, just as you would if it were a hobby.

If a child claims to know a place where you have never been before, this may simply be déja vu, a process in which the mind picks up perceptions seconds before it processes them. Ask the child to show you around. On looking at an old map you may find, for example, that the dead-end they reached was once the entrance to some servants' quarters. If your child does not want to go into a certain place or becomes upset, ignore the inconvenience and take them out immediately. Later ask them quietly why they did not like the place. Try to collect old family photos and take your child to places where their ancestors lived so they get a feeling for their roots.

Don't be offended if your child talks about other parents, but – equally – do not promise that you will take them back to an unidentified place. Explain that children sometimes have memories of what seem to be earlier lives, but they can't go back any more than they can go back to being a baby in a pram. These are just things they can remember.

# CHAPTER 9

# Frightening Psychic Experiences

Negative psychic experiences in childhood are quite rare. Some are a result of the mind externalising underlying – or open – family tensions and the child's fears about them. However, by no means all frightening encounters can be explained away in rational terms, for a perfectly happy child may also be terrified, especially at night, by paranormal activity. Particularly sensitive children and teenagers may occasionally be aware of less positive psychic entities as well as beloved grandmothers and guardian angels. Nevertheless, in spite of what horror films would lead you to believe, children and teenagers are never possessed or harmed by these negative forces. I do not believe that children become evil, although society, inadequate parenting and unwise earthly influences such as violent computer games can lead some to destructive behaviour.

Psychic or psychological, if a child can talk about their paranormal fears and not have them dismissed or ignored, the experiences tend not to recur, or they become less terrifying because they have been shared. Sometimes parents dismiss a child's terror. This may be for the best motives – perhaps because they fear that by acknowledging the child's experience they will fuel the situation. However, this approach is counter-productive, for it leaves the child to deal with their fear alone.

## Alone with their fears

I begin with two accounts in which the child felt isolated by a negative haunting and many years later, as an adult, can still recall the trauma.

Sheila, a medium from Berkshire, England, says that when she was little she was plagued by people in her bedroom – men, women and children – that no one else could see, and would hide under her bedclothes in fear. Now, she says, she realises that this was the beginning of her psychic powers.

When she was five, Sheila used to sit on the step after about six o'clock if her mum was out, as she was too frightened to go in because of all the people inside. She remembers when she was about five seeing an old lady with black robes sitting on her bed and an old man who used to stand in the corner. She was the middle child of five and used to frighten the others so much that eventually she was put in a bedroom on her own. Her mother used to get very cross with her for 'talking such nonsense' and smacked her, so she learned to keep quiet about what she saw. She says she now knows that her father was psychic, but he never mentioned it, as her mother was a very dominant woman.

Sheila thinks it is sad if children see things and, like her, do not have their fears explained. 'If you are afraid of your psychic awareness,' she says, 'your imagination will conjure up all sorts of horrid things.' She was very careful to protect her own children and show them there was nothing to be afraid of, while at the same time encouraging them to have lots of real friends and interests.

For Angela, now in her thirties and a counsellor, the bad psychic experiences went on for years and marred her childhood. Angela was left alone at night from a very early age, and this – not surprisingly – made her fears even worse. She says:

> When I was a child I lived in Japan, Spain, Greece, Cuba, Alabama, Italy and California. My dad is American and was in the US navy, and my mother was Greek. My mother was a strict church-goer and belonged to the Greek Orthodox Church. Though both she and my dad were psychic, she regarded all such things as the work of the devil.
>
> When I lived in Spain and was about three, I saw Jesus on the door of my cupboard. It was my first and most positive experience. I did not tell anyone because my mother would say, 'You have the devil in you', if I mentioned things like that. I cannot remember what Jesus said, but I know he spoke and it was very special.
>
> When I was three or four my parents had left me alone one night. They often left me alone. I was scared of something inside the house, but I could not get out. I was crying and shouting. A neighbour came round and tried to tell me how to unlock the door, but I was too scared of the thing inside. The neighbour had to break a window to get me out. I got in so much trouble.
>
> I was always afraid of what was inside the house, especially at night. In Spain I once stayed with the family of some older friends. They were supposed to be babysitting me, but they went out. In the next room, although I was alone in the house, I could hear breathing. It was a man's breath, heavy and laboured, and it got louder. I was paralysed with fear. The louder it got, the more frightened I became, and then I ran out of the house. It did not follow me. But I got in so much trouble again. From then on I was afraid to stay inside a house alone, as there was always something with me that frightened me.
>
> In California when I was 16 or 17 I used to think if I was on the phone nothing would happen. But one night as I chatted I

became more and more scared. The aunt with whom I was staying collected fridge magnets. She had a huge old-fashioned fridge. Suddenly, every magnet fell off one by one. At boarding school I had a similar experience. I was in our sleeping cabin alone, as my roommate had been suspended. Suddenly the chains on the fold-down table started to rattle.

Once I actually saw the presence. In the US we have a game called Bloody Mary. You stand in the bathroom with the light out looking into the mirror. I was in Greece and about 13. I was in the hotel room where my aunt was staying at the seaside. My cousin and I looked into the mirror and staring back was a man in black in a top hat.

We were terrified, as when I turned round he was still there. We were screaming, and my uncle was banging on the door, but the door would not open. Then the man disappeared and the door opened again.

In California I was sleeping on the floor at a friend's house when a woman in a flowing dress appeared, said, 'Oh, you are here', and floated out. That was the only time I felt calm when I saw a ghost.

Angela still sees presences, but now she has trained psychically and so is no longer afraid. Angela's is an extreme example of how badly handled early psychic experiences can plague a young person for years and leave them afraid at night even when they see nothing.

Hearing breathing is a feature of a number of negative psychic experiences I have collected and may result from the development of clairaudient, or psychic hearing, powers. The breathing itself may not be malevolent, but the young person does not know why they are hearing it.

## Night terrors

Night terrors are different from nightmares (which are simply bad dreams) and occur during a different stage of the sleep cycle: the deepest one, when we should not be awake. With a night terror, the child will wake filled with fear but not know why; they will have no frame of reference (unlike with a nightmare). They will be staring wide-eyed and terrified, and sometimes screaming at something the mother cannot see – and to which they cannot give a name. Night terrors are quite rare and have to do with the physiology of the sleep process. A child may experience sleep paralysis during them and be unable to move.

The psychologist Melanie Klein wrote that at night, when invisible foes seem at their most potent, the child can feel hemmed in by all sorts of malevolent powers, 'sorcerers, witches, devils, phantastic figures and animals as his or her own bad thoughts come back to haunt him'. The most important point about nightmares and night terrors would seem to be that, however improbable they might appear to adults, they should be treated seriously. A child should be able to confide in their parents without fear of being mocked or disbelieved.

One explanation for night terrors given by psychologists is that they are 'eidetic images', pictures that are so vivid in the child's mind that they project them into their surroundings, as a cinema projector throws images on to a screen.

Experiments have been carried out in which a child is shown a picture that is then removed. Some children have the ability to point out details as though the absent picture was still there. It has been claimed that between 30 and 90 per cent of children possess this ability, though recent tests have put the figure as low as 7 per cent. Often the child cannot understand why the adult cannot see what they are seeing.

In the case of night terrors, is the child unconsciously projecting images from their imagination, from a book or from a television programme? This may explain the case of Jane, from Wales, who told me:

> When I was a small child of about two-and-a-half, we were living on a new council estate in Cardiff that had been built on a bomb site. I was lying in bed and I was convinced I could see a face on the wall, the same colour as the plaster but with bright red lips. It was like the Queen's profile on a stamp or a cameo. I remember being absolutely terrified at the time of what the family referred to in later years as my 'Lady Hoo-Hoo' which must have been what I called her when I tried to explain.

Tricia, from Milwaukee, USA, not only had night terrors as a young child but, according to her adoptive mother, would sometimes sleepwalk and cry, saying that she was trying to get out of a big grey door that was stuck. She would always recall the same image when she woke: a white face with a sailor hat pressed against a round thick glass window. Years later, she traced her birth mother and discovered that her natural father had been a sailor. He drowned when his submarine sank during the Second World War. No one had survived, because the water pressure jammed the escape doors. In his dying moments, did he think of the little girl he had never seen?

## Childhood fears

Fears of ghosts often make themselves known at night because the dark frightens many children. Sometimes the presence is unseen but nevertheless felt. Stairs seem to be particularly frightening.

When Sue was very small, she lived in Poole, in England, and remembers feeling a presence on the landing whenever she went upstairs. She says:

It used to chase me down the stairs, and I was terrified. It went on until my father painted the stairs white. It was originally brown varnish.

Stephanie is a teenager who wrote to me through my website.

My scary experience was when I was a kid of about seven or eight, and I was given a wardrobe where the door would not shut. This may sound weird and stupid, but when my mum was not there, I could see a shadow of a cloak and a hood. You could tell it was a cloak.

When I shouted to my mum to come up, it would turn into a door, and then again after she went downstairs I would see the cloaked shape again. This went on for a few days, so I asked my mum to smash up the wardrobe, which she did. She got my uncle to do it. After that I was fine, I never saw the shape again. I am still living in the same house and I do not get scared at all.

In the case of Mark, who lives in Newport, in Wales, it was a chest of drawers that seemed to hold the restless spirit that disturbed his sleep. It may be that impressions from the past do become attached to a particular piece of old furniture. If the furniture was present when a sad event took place, the child may pick up these negative imprints (see also Tim's experience, on page 129). Mark talked to me on a radio phone-in programme.

When I was no more than six, I used to hear the sound of a man breathing in my bedroom. I mentioned it to my mum and dad, and they said it was just my sisters snoring next door, but it wasn't. The sound was different and always came from behind a very old dressing table. It stopped when the family got rid of the dressing table. I mentioned it 20 years later to my sister, and she said she had heard the sound when she had that bedroom, and my other sister had heard it too when she had the room.

The strange thing was, none of us had mentioned it to the others as children. I used to get my torch out from under my pillow and go and investigate. Now I don't know how I had the nerve.

Jenny was 11 and living in Australia when she recounted the following experience that happened to her family while they were living in New Zealand. It is reproduced from the *Scottish Society for Psychical Research Journal* with the permission of Daphne Plowman and of Jenny's mother, Pauline. Jenny writes:

This true story happened in a quiet town called Whangarei in New Zealand.

A little Maori boy woke one night and got out of bed to fetch a glass of milk. What he did not know was that watching him from the dark shadows of the door was a sinister form. He dropped his milk and turned round. All he saw was a pair of red eyes looking at him. The little boy ran through to his mum and dad's bedroom and started shouting and jumping round the room in terror. His mother calmed him and phoned a friend who is a spiritualist medium, my mum Pauline.

Early the next morning my mum went to the Maori house to feel what was there. After some time and lots of prayers, my mother came home.

Later that evening my brother Tod was lying on his bed. When he looked up he saw red eyes looking at him from the shadow of his wardrobe. Tod said it looked a bit like ET and was carrying a stone. It came over to the bed and deliberately dropped the stone in front of Tod. However, as the stone was spirit, it dropped straight through the bed, so the spectre bent down to pick it up.

Tod screamed out for Mum and she came running through to the bedroom. The apparition ran behind the door when Mum came in. Tod saw the short black shadow and told Mum where it was. Mum turned round and saw it looking with its big red eyes. My mother said lots of prayers to get rid of it and finally a big hand came down from the roof and pulled it away. I think it was God's hand coming down and taking the spirit to heaven.

The bad spirit had followed Pauline home. Perhaps he was linked to earlier negative Maori magic practised by *tohunga makutu,* black magic experts, on the site of, or close to, the present home of the little Maori boy. Pauline was an experienced medium. It is tempting when visiting ancient places to try to 'play' at magic, and this is very much encouraged by teenage occult fiction television series and some less responsible paranormal documentaries. However, amateur spook hunters who try to summon up spirits of the past out of curiosity, whether Celtic, Maori, Aboriginal or Native North American, should remember that this means entering a realm of powerful magical powers that the civilised world barely understands. The majority of these powers are totally benign, but in play you may attract less positive energies.

Doreen, from Manchester, England, recalled her terrifying dream experience and how her grandfather helped her:

When I was about four years old I had one of the strangest dreams I ever had. It was in colour (I always dream in colour). It concerned my granddad and myself. My granddad had old-fashioned furniture in his bedroom. The bed was very high, and there was a double wardrobe in the corner. He worked nights, so after waving him off I was taken to bed.

As normal, I fell into a deep sleep. In my dream I was lying in my granddad's bed. I saw him lying on the other side of the bed, very still. 'Hiya, Granddad,' I said, but he said nothing.

Just then I heard a tell-tale creak of the wardrobe door opening. I watched in horror as different-coloured stick men with pointed heads came marching out of the wardrobe and disappeared under the bed. Then they started poking their pointed heads through the bed, the mattress and my granddad. As I looked at Granddad, he turned his head and said, 'It's all right, love.'

My dad came and woke me up. We went downstairs and I was told my granddad had been in an accident at work and had died. I cried and said he could not be dead because I had seen him in bed and he had spoken to me and told me he was all right. My dad took me upstairs to Granddad's bed, and of course he was not there. He had fallen off a 30-foot [10-metre] crane and died instantly.

## A brutal reaction to a child's terror

This account, from Peter, who lives in Dorset, England, is one of the saddest experiences I have come across. I am telling it because it is true and shows how a sensitive child was brutalised because of his psychic terrors. I have changed the names and location by request.

My first recollection of anything out of the ordinary was when I was 11 years old and we had moved home on the day the Second World War had ended to the little town of Christchurch. We had only been there a few days when I had my first nightmare.

I dreamed that I was standing at the edge of a large area of close-mown grass and that there was a track leading across it to a river, made by people walking along the same route until a path was worn into the grass. A derelict metal boat was tied to the river bank, and it was to the boat the path led.

In my nightmare it was night. The sky was lit by a huge yellow moon, and every now and then a heavy dark cloud would obscure it, and it would become completely dark. I was terrified and tried to run from this place, which I sensed was evil, but I was unable to do so. It seemed as though someone or something was controlling me and forcing me to walk across the path towards the ship.

The nearer I got to the ship, the more my terror grew. Every time the clouds hid the moon, I would stop and wait for the path to be illuminated again and then continue on my way. Finally I reached the ship. There was a plank of wood leading from the bank to the boat, and I was forced to cross over. All the time I was trying to run, trying to cry out but was unable to do either.

On the deck was a hatchway with some steps leading down below the deck. I walked down these steps and found myself in what looked like a corridor. There were four doors either side and one door at the end facing me. I started to walk along the corridor. Each of the doors on either side was open, completely smashed or missing. I was not really aware of them. I felt I was being drawn to the door facing me, the only one that was shut. When I reached it, I found that it had been tied shut with a piece of thin rope. I undid the rope and the angle of the ship caused the door to swing wide open.

At this time the moon was free of cloud, and the room was well lit through the various holes in the deck and sides of the ship. I had a momentary glimpse of the room, like being shown a black-and-white photograph for a split second, but the picture is as clear today as it was then, over 50 years ago.

Directly in front of me was a broken table. One of the legs had been broken from it and was lying on the floor. In the far right-hand corner was a length of thick, heavy-looking rope. As I said, I had a momentary glimpse of all this, and then it appeared. The far left-hand corner was in shadow, but in the shadow was something that was darker than the shadow. There was no shape to it. It was just a shadow, darker than the shadows.

The thing rose up, getting larger as it did so. Eventually, it filled the room, towering above me. Then it swooped down and enveloped me. I felt I was being suffocated. There was a horrible smell. I could taste a foul mustiness. At this point I screamed and screamed and screamed.

The next thing I knew I was in bed. The light was switched on and I was given a thrashing for daring to wake up my parents.

The frightening thing about this, apart from the nightmare, was that I had this dream every time there was bright moonlight. My father took a sadistic delight in telling me that I was going insane. The word lunatic, he told me, came from the name of the moon, luna. He said I was mad and would eventually be locked up in a lunatic asylum.

I must have had this nightmare a dozen times or more, being soundly beaten each time for daring to disturb my parents. Then it was finally decided that I should see a doctor. In the practice my parents had registered with was a Doctor Kaye. The doctor fancied herself as something of a psychologist and I was duly taken to see her.

I was told to describe the setting of my nightmare in as much detail as possible. I was then asked if I had been to Christchurch Harbour. At this time I had not even started my new school and not been allowed out to play, so for the time I had been in Christchurch I had not been further than the shops across the road. The harbour was about three miles away. I did not even know there was a harbour.

Doctor Kaye told my parents I had given a perfect description of Christchurch Harbour and that the metal boat I had seen in my dream did, in fact, exist. Three boats had been tied up in the harbour. One was a huge tea boat that used to take people out for high tea in the harbour. This was derelict, stuck in the mud and falling apart with decay. Then there were two minesweepers, relics of the war in the Atlantic. One was made of wood, and one was made of metal. These two boats were tied up at the far side of the river and they were inaccessible except by boat.

Doctor Kaye explained that a couple of weeks after my nightmares had started, there had been a terrific storm. The tea boat and the wooden boat had been broken up and washed away. The metal minesweeper had been torn from the moorings on the far side of the river and was grounded against the bank on the side nearest to us. Someone had placed a wooden plank from the bank to the deck of the boat. In my nightmare I had seen Christchurch harbour exactly as it was, but my nightmares had started before the storm that changed the position of the boat. As I said earlier, I had never been there.

Doctor Kaye then came up with a suggestion that she and my parents thought was a good idea. I would be taken to the harbour and made to walk across the grass to the boat to see how stupid my nightmares really were. Accordingly, a couple of nights later, Doctor Kaye came round at about 8 pm to collect me with my mother, and we went to the harbour. Whether by accident or design, there was an almost full moon. The doctor and my mother stayed on the edge of the grass and I was told to walk to the ship.

The moment I started to walk towards the ship, the nightmare came alive. It was almost as if I was in a trance and couldn't stop walking and I couldn't even cry out. Some force seemed to be drawing me forward. I felt the same terrors as in my nightmare. The fact that my mother and the doctor were a few yards away made absolutely no difference. I was literally in my nightmare. I reached the plank and started to cross the deck of the ship, still trying desperately to run or cry out.

I think that my terror was even greater here than in my nightmare because this time I knew it was happening for real. In front of me was a hatch with steps leading down below the deck exactly as I had seen in the dream. Unable to stop, I went down the steps and found myself in the corridor I had dreamed about. There was a slight difference, however. Although, as in the nightmare, there were four rooms either side and a closed door facing me at the end, there were no doors to any of the rooms on either side. They were all broken inside the rooms, and some of the wood had been used to make fires. I eventually reached the end door. The piece of cord that tied it had been undone and was hanging down from the door. I pushed the door open. I tried to close my eyes so as not to see what was in the room but was unable to do so.

In front of me was a broken table. Behind it was a broken chair. It looked as if someone had unsuccessfully tried to make a fire with it. To the right of me was a pile of rags and a piece of thick rope and then the shadow in the corner materialised. The corner was quite dark, but the shadow was darker. I tried to look away but was not able to do so. The shadow rose up until it filled the whole room and then it towered over me and began to enfold me. I could feel it slowly covering my body and I managed to scream and scream and then everything went black.

The next thing I remember was waking up in bed and it was daylight. For a moment I thought I had just had another nightmare and had overslept. I jumped out of bed and fell flat on my face. My mother came in and I got the usual clout round the ear for being a nuisance. She told me that the doctor had given me something to calm me down and to make me sleep to get over the fit I had had on the boat.

All she could tell me was that they had followed me a little way and waited by the boat for me to return. I started screaming suddenly and went into some sort of fit. The doctor was annoyed because she missed the plank in her hurry to get to me and went up to her knees in mud. When they finally found me, I was unconscious. I was kept under sedation for three days.

Doctor Kaye suggested that the spirit of one of the seamen who had died on the boat had been unable to find rest and had found me a receptive medium. This does not explain the pure evil I felt emanating from the shadow. But after the visit to the boat I never had the nightmare again.

It is to be hoped that no psychic experience would be dealt with in this way today. Peter still bears the scars of these incidents and has had a number of other bad psychic experiences as an adult.

### Ghosts and earthly trauma

As I have said, we should not be too ready to blame ghostly activity on family stress. Indeed, paranormal activity may, if not tackled positively, create or exacerbate family tensions.

Marian, whom I met in Oxford, England, told me the following story of a little girl called Sarah who was four-and-a-half years old and lived in Frome, Somerset. Sarah was her friend Gill's daughter.

Sarah's dad walked out of the family home and left the area after years of family tension. Shortly afterwards, Gill and Sarah were rehoused by the local council in a house that was vacant because the 80-year-old man who had previously lived there had died.

Then Sarah started seeing an old man. He used to sit on a chair in her bedroom. It wasn't the presence that frightened Sarah but his refusal to respond to her when she spoke. Her grandparents were the first to hear of Sarah's 'old man'. They spoke to neighbours and found that Sarah's description of the old man tallied exactly with the appearance of the previous tenant.

Visits to doctors followed but to no avail, until at last the family contacted a psychotherapist who was sympathetic to alternative ideas. The psychotherapist advised Gill that Sarah should have plenty of opportunities to talk about the old man and her fears and be reassured that she was special and that the old man only wanted to be sure that the new family was looking after the house he had lived in and loved for most of his life.

Marian gave the family a copy of an earlier edition of this book, which confirmed that lots of other families had had similar experiences, especially in times of trouble, and Sarah's family weren't bad, mad or odd. The family used the book as a basis to talk things over.

The old man's visits became fewer, maybe as a result of all the tensions being brought out in the open. They stopped completely once Sarah started school. There certainly was a psychological element to Sarah's experience, but it can't be dismissed as imagination because the old man Sarah saw was exactly like the old man who had lived in the house.

Jessica, a teacher in Hertfordshire, England, told me about her dilemma concerning two pupils' experiences in which the paranormal activity was a manifestation of stress but still paranormal.

A family came to the school whom we heard had had a lot of trouble with the police where they used to live, mainly involving some cousins. The oldest boy, Tim, who was eight and in my class, seemed very tense and behaved oddly. Then he started to draw ghosts and to talk about a thing in his house that threw plates and smashed things.

Tim became progressively more afraid of what was happening at home. I didn't know what to do and so I tried to talk to the headmistress about the problem. But she told me on no account must I encourage Tim to talk about what was happening and that I should change the subject if he mentioned it. I didn't want to go against her, but I kept an eye on the lad. Things got worse at home and so did his behaviour. I wonder if we should have intervened.

One morning he told me that a vicar had been to the house and the thing had gone. Tim's behaviour improved dramatically. But now I have Jimmy, Tim's younger brother, in my class and recently he has become tense and difficult. Jimmy too has started to draw ghosts, and I don't know what to do. We were concerned to hear that the four children had been locked in their room, and I know there has been violence in the family. But no one will talk about the poltergeist, though I fear it is starting up again.

Jodie was seven and living in Surrey, England, when things started flying out of her wardrobe and hitting her. She was convinced there was a demon with black eyes that came out at night, and she refused to go to bed. Her mother, Linda, was at the end of her tether. Linda had remarried a year before and had a new baby to cope with. But Jodie's poltergeist couldn't be explained away as attention-seeking, because it was terrifying the child.

Fortunately, Linda didn't tell Jodie she was being silly. Instead, she moved Jodie's bed into the baby's bedroom. She spent time in the old bedroom with Jodie during the day and even took the door off the wardrobe, as it was carved and quite scary. She encouraged Jodie to help her rearrange the furniture and choose new curtains. Finally, Jodie moved back in, keeping a nightlight burning and a 'magic bell' to call Linda if she was afraid. Linda made sure Jodie had plenty of attention when the baby was asleep, and the poltergeist disappeared. Whether or not the psychic attack was triggered by jealousy of the baby matters little: the problem was resolved.

## Poltergeists

The activities of poltergeists, the noisy ghosts who are alleged to cause so much disruption in houses, are often linked with teenagers, though – as the previous case demonstrates – poltergeist activity can also occur around younger children who are under stress.

Psychokinetic energy, or the power of a mind consciously or unconsciously to move objects without touching them, may be emitted by an adolescent child. This energy can cause plates to fly and ornaments to shatter. The release of psychokinetic energy is usually caused by general family stress. When, for example, a violent quarrel occurs between parents or a simmering resentment comes to a head, the build-up of psychic energy in one or more children present is ignited by the parental anger or stress.

Of all psychic activities, poltergeist visitation is the one that most indicates that the child and the family need support, not judgement. A problem may arise if the child alone is blamed for causing the disturbance and is treated as a scapegoat, whereas in fact the whole family is unconsciously implicated and the child rarely, if ever, knows they are releasing psychic energy. The child involved, often a young teenager, especially needs sympathetic treatment. Sensationalist films such as *Carrie*, in which a girl destroys people with her mind power, are pure fantasy and counter-productive to a sensible approach to poltergeist activity.

Poltergeist activity often ceases when a parent or other family member leaves a warring household and the family crisis diminishes.

A very disturbing case occurred some years ago, in which an eight-year-old boy in a town in southern England was rejected by his foster parents because he was blamed for bringing a poltergeist upon them. I will call the child concerned Kenny. He will now be grown-up and hopefully happy and settled after an incident that was in no way his fault.

Kenny's first foster mother suffered from a progressive illness, and the boy was diagnosed as having learning difficulties – sometimes regarded as a significant factor in poltergeist cases (or it may be that children with learning and behavioural difficulties are less able to explain what is really happening to them).

There was considerable disturbance in the house: bookcases spilling books, china smashing, and a medium called in by a social worker identified the presence of a boy called Don, who said he played with Kenny in the garden. The medium linked Don with a young down-and-out who had died in the area.

The foster father reported that Kenny did say he was playing with a boy called Don who had a bicycle when there was apparently no one there with him. However, a newspaper reporter pointed out that there was a real Don with a bicycle who lived nearby and who Kenny sometimes played with.

This latter information was ignored, and the neighbourhood's self-styled white witch brought the situation to boiling point by pinpointing the source of 'the malevolent force' as the unfortunate boy, apparently because of some unspecified early trauma in his life. She felt that if Kenny were removed, everything would be fine. So the lad was removed and the activity ceased (although apparently no psychic phenomena occurred at his new home).

Whatever the true version of events, it is a sad indictment of those involved in the case that it was the child, perhaps the person most in need of help, who was seen as the cause of the problem and was the one to suffer.

Phil is now in his early twenties. At the time he told me of this experience he was a teenager living with foster parents in the south of England. The trouble began when his mother remarried and his new stepfather moved in.

> Every night we could hear a creaking noise coming from the loft. Mum thought it might be wind, but the noise happened even when there was no wind. My step-dad went into the loft and found an old chair rocking by itself. He saw a white figure move across the window.
>
> Then, when we were having dinner, plates would start being thrown around by themselves. Mum was really scared, so she got the local vicar in. He came quite a few times and said it would be all right, but after he went, the noises would always come back.
>
> We started to sleep downstairs, because it was so scary. At last my step-dad got the rocking chair from the loft. I was hiding under the covers, but the chair flew out of his hands and threw my step-dad on to my bed. The chair landed on me and really hurt me.
>
> My step-dad threw the chair on to a bonfire but it did no good. Things kept flying around and breaking, so in the end we moved out of the house. But I am now living with foster parents because my step-dad used to hurt me.

Jane is a computer analyst. She grew up in a cottage in north Warwickshire, England, with her mum, dad and elder sister. When Jane was 11, she woke one night and saw an old man sitting on the end of her bed, but she wasn't frightened. She smiled at him and he smiled back. The old man had a cap, a stick and piercing blue eyes.

Unusually, Jane's parents didn't laugh at what they called her vivid imagination. They looked shocked when she described the old man, although they wouldn't say why. It wasn't until years later that Jane found out she had seen the previous owner of the house, who had died in what was now her room.

Jane's parents had been experiencing problems in their marriage for some time, and there had been many late-night arguments. Her sister spent a lot of time away from the family, so Jane felt very isolated with the family troubles. If there was an unhappy atmosphere when she sat down to breakfast, plates and ornaments would start to move. Her parents accused her of playing tricks, but Jane was frightened, and became even more so as her parents' marriage deteriorated.

One evening, when everyone was in the kitchen, the family heard footsteps coming downstairs. Jane had heard footsteps in the middle of the night when she was younger, but her parents had told her she was dreaming. This time even her father was scared. It was the first time the family admitted that there might be something haunting them.

In spite of this, Jane's parents took her to various psychiatrists and therapists, who all suggested that she was trying to punish her parents by playing tricks on them. Jane became more and more nervous and developed anorexia. Her experiences were explained as symptoms of her eating problems.

The paranormal activity stopped when Jane's mother left home.

We don't understand fully how the psychic and the psychological interact in such cases, but we can be sure that the child is subconsciously saying that they feel attacked by what is going on in the family.

### Pure psychic attack

Dave, aged 15, had a happy settled home life, yet also had a poltergeist in his new house, built on what was formerly priory land. The poltergeist was creating disturbances in the house long before Dave reached adolescence. His parents slept downstairs and seemed to have no problems in their room. However, when Dave's father was sitting in the bath one night, the shower suddenly exploded, sending glass from the cabinet flying everywhere and cutting him quite badly. The shower was not in use at the time. Dave's younger sister, Sarah, often heard voices and strange noises in her room, and when Dave's friend, Robert, slept in the room, he could hear breathing from the corner, which terrified him.

One night Jane, Dave's girlfriend, slept in Dave's room while he slept downstairs. She woke in the early hours of the morning to see a dark misty figure standing next to her bed. Unwilling to call out and wake the household, she turned to face the wall, and in the morning the figure was gone. On another occasion, the small red light on Dave's hi-fi, on the other side of the room, grew larger and moved closer and closer until it was floating in front of her. On yet another occasion, Dave was alone in the house and phoning Jane when suddenly all the plates flew out of the cupboard and smashed. Dave was terrified. Several times, when there had been no one upstairs, doors that had been left closed were opened. Although Jane and Dave closed them again, before long they were once more open.

Dave's house would seem to be haunted independently of the teenager/poltergeist interaction. Adolescents, like young children, are known to be more sensitive to the existence of phantoms and paranormal activity. Equally, ghosts and poltergeists may interact more with sensitive teenagers because they are of an age at which they are more open and receptive, their identity once again very fluid, as in early childhood.

## Teenage fears of evil

Negative psychic experiences are generally most common in adolescence. The physical and emotional changes as well as the challenges of life away form the security of parental protection unsettle some teenagers' psyches. This can also be the time when they dabble with ouija boards, watch nasty occult films and scare themselves. I have described such instances on page 159. Above all, the awareness of evil in the world can cause teenagers to question the nature of humanity. And as ever bloodier scenes appear on television news, and nastier programmes are shown before the 9 pm watershed, I have noticed that these formerly teenage-type encounters with evil experiences are also occurring with increasing frequency among younger children.

As I have said, I do not believe that evil spirits can possess a child or adolescent, but if a spirit was dominant in their earthly life, they may try to play mind games with someone they knew and bullied when alive.

Annette is a mother of two and lives in Victoria, Australia. She still sees the ghost of her childhood friend Lee, who was killed in a road accident. Both Annette and Lee were partially deaf, so they enjoyed a special form of non-verbal communication – which can be more powerful in some ways than words. Annette described how after Lee's death she was terrified by a vision in the mirror.

Lee died from massive head injuries after she went through the windscreen of a car. I went to school with her. One morning not long after her death, I looked in my mirror and I could see Lee's face. She was wearing her very sarcastic expression. When Lee was alive she could be overpowering.

She would look into my eyes, and I could see the determination in hers. To us, eye contact was a different way of talking. About six months before her death, I found if you blinked it broke the spell, and she hated that because she always wanted to be top dog.

I suppose with Lee I'd always thought she could do better than me – talk more, speak more clearly and act in a more adult way. Lee was always carefree and lived it up. But two weeks before she died, she had enrolled as a nurse for old people – that was her greatest ambition – and seemed to be settling down.

I've seen Lee in the mirror several times since she died, her face over mine as though she was trying to take me over. I know it would be so easy for me to let her spirit into my body, but I know her too well. I wouldn't be strong enough to control her.

Annette used the paranormal experience to assert her independence from Lee. It is a battle Annette would have had to fight on the earthly plane had Lee lived.

Teenagers' growing intellectual abilities do not necessarily make them less vulnerable to frightening experiences. Teenagers know more of the dark side of life than young children do, and yet do not have the reassurance that wise adults can put it all right. They see the questions and cannot find the answers.

Gina, from Surrey, England, was brought up by a Muslim father and a Christian mother. At the age of 16, she wrote:

I remember as a child talking to God quite frequently because I was afraid of my parents. They hit me. I found God was the only person I could talk to for help, and it was quite comforting to know or believe there was someone there to help and look after me. I think this belief enabled me to have contact with a power.

Ever since that day, I have seen presences in the house. I have had powers shout my name so piercingly in my head that I have become very afraid.

I cannot contain these powers and I cannot force them to do anything for me or for anyone. I have written to clairvoyants, and they have told me I have a gift that will develop. I tried to tell my mother. She said, 'Yes, dear', and never took it further.

Gina's voices may well represent many underlying fears about her life in a mixed-culture family where she feels torn apart emotionally.

## Demonic encounters

Though we know that the devil is a Judeo–Christian creation, teenagers – especially after watching scary Satan-type films – can become afraid of an evil force taking them over. Often they do see the devil figure in the way he was traditionally portrayed from the fourth century CE onwards, as half goat or ram with horns and cloven hooves. This depiction was in fact an attempt by the Church fathers to demonise the pre-Christian horned god of the animals that was and still is a feature of indigenous hunting societies. He was also based on the Graeco–Roman goat god of nature, Pan. This is the image still imprinted by some more formal branches of the Church and has become a stereotype of evil even among those of no faith.

Experiences of being crushed by a demonic figure are common, especially among older teenage girls and women in their twenties or even early thirties, and may be partly rooted in fears about their own awakening sexual powers. The mystic Thomas Aquinas wrote in his thirteenth-century book *Summa Theologica* about incubi, sexual demons who plagued young women. However, by no means all of these the modern-day attacks are sexual and many are more to do with fears of powerlessness.

Jill, from Berkshire, England, now married with a family of her own, told me this incident from her childhood.

I was always scared of the back bedroom where I used to sleep. We moved to the house when I was 11. The main thing I noticed was that it was always freezing in there.

I had a friend to stay not long after we moved. We had single beds quite a way apart. I woke up in the night and the bed was shaking. I got up and it carried on shaking. My friend woke up too and her bed was shaking. She remembered it years later. I told my parents and they said, 'It's because we live near the railway.' But we were about half a mile (1 kilometre) from the track, which was on the other side of the house. It was the only time it happened in the six years we were at the house, and it didn't happen in my friend's house and she lived next door.

When I was 13 or 14, I started to have a dream about an upsidedown cross. We weren't a religious family and never went to church. I was horrified to be told by my friends that it was to do with the devil. Not long after, I had an awful vision of the devil. He had huge horns like a ram and a horrible face. His face was dark and half ram, half human.

I don't believe in the devil now, but I had no doubt then. I think I said a prayer. I felt a physical force. He was trying to crush me. I was absolutely terrified. It lasted ten or 15 seconds I suppose, but it was like eternity.

My parents took no notice. They always said it was my imagination. They were strong people who did not show emotion.

Jill went to a doctor for help and he advised her to recite the Lord's Prayer.

Janet, who lives in Bracknell, England, is now in her early forties but can still recall the demon that terrified her as a teenager.

> When I was about 16, I had an experience that frightened the life out of me. I woke to find a heaving weight on my chest, choking the life from my body. The room was freezing. I could see the dent on the bed that this invisible force was making and I was fighting to breathe as it grasped me and pressed my neck till I thought I would suffocate. At last it went suddenly, leaving me shaking and exhausted.
>
> This happened on two occasions. The second time, I said the Lord's Prayer and the fiend, as I thought of it, never came back.

A strong Christian faith cannot always provide protection against apparent manifestations of evil. It may be that it provides an even more tempting target for such forces, because natural desires and the fear of sin may be in conflict. Andrea, from Somerset, England, wrote:

> When I was 17, I had an experience during Lent. Being the regular church organist and piano player, I was asked to play for four consecutive Tuesday evening services. On the second evening, before starting the service, I sat at the piano rehearsing a few hymns with the congregation in the church hall where the service was being held.
>
> Upon practising the last hymn, I casually peered over to the front doors — I presume I was expecting to see any late arrivals — but a kind of woman was staring in at me, expressionless, with no features; dead, white flesh, with a black scarf of some kind which went all round her head. I went dizzy and my heart beat fast, but I just couldn't tear my eyes away from it. I looked away but had to look again and finally let out a loud gasp. Everyone shut up suddenly and the vicar asked what was wrong.
>
> For some unknown reason, I said I thought I'd seen my dead grandmother. Why I said that I don't know, but what I'd seen was unexplicable. During the peace, the vicar's wife came over to comfort me and said that Satan tries to destroy church services. My playing the piano made me a target.
>
> On the last Sunday evening, at the service again, I suddenly sensed a frightening sensation during the start of the service. I didn't dare turn round to the front doors, but I asked the vicar to pray, and he cleared the church hall and asked whatever was bad to go. After that I felt a lot better.

Whether Andrea saw the devil or a manifestation of her fears of being possessed, we do not know. A sense of powerlessness, felt by many teenagers, can be as strong as a fear of being possessed.

It is not only girls who confront such forces in adolescence. Anna, an experienced religious education teacher, told me that a 15-year-old boy in her class confided in her that when he looked in the mirror he saw the face of the devil over his shoulder.

> He was frightened, as he couldn't talk to his parents about it, and asked me what he should do. I suggested he might think of something good and substitute it for the bad thing that was terrifying him. I didn't know how else to help. It seemed to work, but I wondered if he had other problems he felt he couldn't share.

## Self-induced terrors

There is no greater danger for young people than using ouija boards or conjuring up spirits in séances. The effects on the mind are every bit as severe as the possible psychic dangers. No loving, deceased relative or spirit guardian would be summoned up by what is a dangerous party game. I know of children as young as nine playing with ouija boards (whereas this used to be the pursuit of young teenagers), because of the cult vampire television series in which spirits and demons can be summoned at will by magic. There are also joke voodoo sets sold even in some responsible bookstores that can lead to nasty mind games. The following are just three stories that typify the problem.

Pat, from Berkshire, England, told me that when her daughter Franny was about 12, she and some of her friends had been playing with a ouija board in the school cloakroom at lunchtime after Franny found a book about ouija boards in the school library. Franny believes she picked up a spirit, because she started to be haunted by an old man. Pat told me: 'He used to sit on her dressing table. He followed her all the time. He used to just sit there watching her. It was horrifying.'

One night when Pat's husband was at work, things got so bad that Pat rang their Catholic priest, but he was out. Pam says: 'My daughter was completely hysterical. I talked to her to calm her, and we sprinkled holy water around her room. After that it seemed to quieten down. I made her promise never to fool around with a ouija board again.'

Ashi went to an exclusive convent school in the Home Counties of England and had dabbled with the ouija board during the lunchtime break in the classroom from the age of 14. When Ashi was 16, she and her best friend, Ally, were playing with the board. Ashi told me:

> It was a time when school friendships are the centre of your world and you can't imagine it being otherwise. So Ally asked the glass, 'Will Ashi and I always be friends?'
>
> 'No.'
>
> 'Why not?'
>
> 'Dead. Car.'

Ally was very upset, and they stopped doing the ouija board after that. But six months later, almost to the day, Ally was killed in a car crash. It may well have been a coincidence, but the experience upset Ashi for many years.

Pam from Birmingham, England, had tried to talk to her mum about ghosts because the subject fascinated her, but her mother told her that psychism was rubbish. When Pam was 14, she started to use the ouija board at school with her friends. Pam was specially singled out for nice messages, to her friends' annoyance, and they accused her of cheating. The spirit told her she'd meet a new boyfriend called John. This was not unlikely, since John is such a common name, and, as a result of this information, Pam would have been unconsciously giving out positive vibes to every John she met after the séance. The spirit also promised that she'd do well in her end-of-term exams. Pam had worked hard all year, but when her results were good, she was convinced that her success was due to the spirit on the board.

Then the glass told Pam she had a great psychic gift, so she started to play with lexicon letters at home alone. But things turned nasty. The spirit said that her best friend Jan was jealous and was saying nasty things behind her back. Pam caught Jan whispering to another girl in the cloakroom, and after a terrible row, Pam and Jan stopped speaking to each other. Then the glass warned her that if she went dancing there would be a fire at the disco that would disfigure her face. The spirit refused to say when this would happen, so Pam gave up going to discos even at school. The next week, the spirit told her that the school bus would crash, but again gave no time. Pam was terrified and refused to go to school.

Pam's mother, noticing that Pam was behaving strangely, finally confronted her and asked if she had been taking drugs. Pam confessed to using a ouija board, and her mother called in the local priest. They destroyed the cards and blessed Pam's bedroom.

Pam's mother felt guilty that she'd not allowed her daughter to talk about the psychic when she was first interested in it and that she had found it easier to suspect her daughter of taking drugs than of dabbling in the occult.

Teenage experiments are very common, and it's only by bringing the psychic out into the open that a parent can divest the darker aspects of their mystique and glamour.

### Earthly support

Worryingly, sensitive teenagers such as Gina, whose experience I described on page 156, can be encouraged by postal or e-mail clairvoyants, some of whom may have no interest in psychism but a great deal of interest in making money. Some such clairvoyants can be dangerous.

I recently met an older teenager, Mona, who came 300 kilometres (180 miles) to see me when I was in Sweden, because she had been told by a medium from abroad that she had black magic round her. Not surprisingly, the medium had asked for money to remove the curse. I hope I was able to reassure Mona.

Helga lives in Holland. She wrote to me via my website because she felt she was being taken over by an older woman who claimed to have spiritual powers.

> I have had psychic abilities from my childhood onwards. In my search for other people like me I met a lot of different individuals. One of them is a Reiki master. For years now she has been doing things with me on an astral plane in order to make me cooperate with her plans (this she admits). Every time she does this, I feel very weak, and I often have a lot of pain in my body too. I asked her to stop, but she says it is for the best, to open me. I know this can't be right. Please can you advise me how to stop this. I am tired of protecting myself all the time. I sometimes use an energy field around me, but whenever I neglect it, I am her prey again.

I wrote back with some suggestions, and Helga replied:

> I thank you sincerely for the advice you gave me. Thank you also for the protection you sent. It feels so good, so calming. You also give me the advice to confide in my mother or in another older person. My mother does not want to know about my psychic abilities. I sense it frightens her, so I don't ever tell her about it. The Reiki master I wrote to you about claims we are twin souls, which I doubt. I think that if twin souls exist, they at least feel comfortable in the presence of one another. There is no older person that I know of in my neighbourhood that I can confide in about my problems with the Reiki master. She is convinced that I have to work with her. Being with her, however, does not feel right to me.
>
> The main reason is because she wants me to channel, as this is what people often ask her for, someone to give them soul messages. She claims I have to do this for a large public, for a lot of people. I know it is not right to force someone into doing what you want them to do, whether this person wants to or not. And that is exactly what she is trying to do, using Reiki in order to make me do what she wants me to do.
>
> Whenever I feel sick and very weak because of it, she claims that working with her is the only right thing that can save me from becoming more ill or even worse [those were her words].

This is just one of the many requests for help I get from young people who are being manipulated. Almost all Reiki healers are good people and many do wonderful work, but some people do claim power in the name of spirituality, and this can be a form of real abuse. Young people often don't have the earthly support to resist those who wish to take advantage of them. I do try to help long-distance, but am aware that Helga and the others need someone at hand who is experienced in dealing with such matters.

## When a child has a negative psychic experiences

Hard though it is to monitor the kinds of websites, films and television young people watch, try to spend some time sharing good-quality television programmes with them and discuss without prejudice some of the nastier programmes on offer.

Food additives and junk food hype up sensitive children psychically as well as psychologically, so keep food natural if your child is jittery or having a lot of nightmares. You should also cut down on your child's use of computers and mobile phones. Electronic impulses can be disturbing and also discourage the kind of direct communication that defuses psychokinetic energy.

Fear of the dark is quite common even among teenagers and adults. Compromise with hall lights and nightlights. Forcing a child to accept darkness is usually counter-productive. The child may lie silently terrified, especially if they feel like a baby for making a fuss.

In strange houses or hotels or if someone is looking after your child overnight, show the child where the light switches are, discuss any anxieties and make sure you are confident in your sitter. Because we are all so pressurised for time these days, childcare can be difficult – I have had to jump through hoops to get cover sometimes. Try to have emergency sitters who the child trusts – perhaps for whom you can reciprocate the favour.

If your child talks about a frightening ghost at night, don't panic and don't go into denial – sometimes the initial response when our child is upset. Talk through the experience. If you can see any obvious earthly explanations, for example clanking pipes, hinges that need oiling or neighbours with adjoining stairs, tactfully suggest them without minimising the reality of the experience to the child. Reassure the child that nothing paranormal can harm them and ask them what they would like you to do to help them sort out the problem. If it makes the child feel better, allow them to sprinkle the room with sacred water. This is water into which three pinches of sea salt have been stirred with a silver-coloured knife and which has had the sign of the cross made on the surface. Alternatively, buy some from a holy well. Allow the child to choose a small crystal angel or amethyst or rose quartz crystal to act as a symbol of protection that they can hold when they are afraid.

Children are not possessed by evil, but if your child is behaving oddly, tactfully ask if they have been experimenting with an ouija board or calling up spirits. Explain they have not done anything wrong but that dabbling with unknown spirits is just as unwise as inviting strangers into the home.

Try to answer your child's questions about death, evil and suffering in the world as honestly as you can, but do not be afraid to admit that you do not have all the answers.

Should you have a poltergeist, pay attention to what is going on in family life and try to make quiet times for the family when the family can be together and in which no controversial issues may be raised. Listen to your child's worries but accept that none of us is perfect. Marriage breakdowns and homes made tense by debt or career demands do occur, and children are very resilient as long as they know everything that is going on and why.

Above all, if your child is corresponding with an older psychic or is learning healing, make sure that the influence is desirable and non-manipulative. This is especially important if your teenager is very secretive about what they do.

# CHAPTER 10

# Growing up in a Psychic Environment

For this final chapter, I have talked to people who were brought up in a psychic household or grew up totally free with nature. These are people who developed a childhood psychic gift and went on to become professional healers or clairvoyants. All of them have grown into stable, happy successful adults who have an open-minded approach to life and a respect for the natural world.

## The granddaughter of a South American wise woman

Adela lives in Glasgow and is in her late thirties. She grew up in Chile, where the worlds of religion and magic are happily intermingled.

> When I was little my grandmother would tell me special stories. Everyone loved her and she took me everywhere with her. I remember she used to take me to see a wise woman, a friend of hers, who lived not far away on the older side of Santiago in a big colonial house.
>
> The wise woman would do Tarot readings and healing, and she would perform Indian/Catholic blessings for individuals to give them health and protection.
>
> I used to lie on the bed in her house and smell the incense. It was a massive bed, and in the room were beautiful objects and huge crystals. Her prayers were a mixture of Catholicism and the older religions. The Catholic priest knew the good work she did and did not mind. She had holy water and would sprinkle it on my face, and I would get wet, which I thought was funny. She and Granny would pray together for my health and safety. The wise woman put beautiful scented oils on my feet, palms and what I later discovered was my psychic third eye, in the centre of my brow. She made the medicine so it was a gold colour. I was so excited I had a gold fingerprint on my forehead.
>
> Granny and I went three times a year, and the wise woman would bless me. Then she would talk to my granny. She was large and wore very bright clothes, greens, yellows and reds. She had big green eyes and her hair tied back. She wore lots of jewellery. She was very fair. In contrast, my grandmother had olive skin and was very small. Her friend was louder, very charismatic and fascinated

me. Granny always wore black and grey and looked typically South American.

Granny used to read cocoa leaves, and a lot of people came to our house to consult her. If extra help was needed, she would send them on to her friend or they would help them together. As a child, my grandmother had lived in north Chile, where there was a lot of Inca lore. Her parents ran a hotel, and she came across lots of Native South Americans, listened to their stories and learned their healing ways.

Grandma and her friend would also bless people's houses. If someone moved to a new house and it felt spooky, they would either get the priest or Granny to bless it. My granny and her friend would use holy water, made with salt and water, and would open all the windows to get the negative energies out.

My grandmother would detect areas in the house where things were not right and would know before anyone told her that there had been an accident there years previously. Sometimes the people in the house had not known about a tragedy, just that it felt bad.

My grandmother respected the dead and taught our family to do so as well. We treated them as though they were always there. I was never scared of death or ghosts. Even when I was little I knew it was okay. I knew I would always be there. I never saw the dead as haunting us. Dead people were part of our family. We could talk to them, joke with them, and they would tell us off if we were naughty.

My deceased grandfather would wander happily around our house and wherever we lived would come with us. Granny used to talk to my grandfather, but it was never spooky. I could always feel him in the room, and he was kind and loving. We lived with spirits and could sense if it was not a member of the family and should not be there. Granny would direct them on their way.

Once, when we were living in Spain, I was about ten and told a girl visitor, who saw him and was scared, that he would not harm her because he was dead. She told people at school, and they said I was mad. I realised I must not tell anybody outside the family.

My grandmother could change people's luck for the better. In Chile the door of our house was always open because it was very hot. People would just come in and out and sometimes would ask my grandmother for lucky pigs. She made them out of whole lemons with herbs inside and matchstick legs. The people would burn the lemon pig for good luck.

When we had to leave Chile because political problems made it no longer safe, Granny carried a pot of earth with her to Glasgow and kept it for years. On special occasions, we would touch the soil to connect us with our homeland. It was part of us. She never went home and to our sorrow was not buried in her beloved native soil. However, we have done ceremonies there when we have been able to return.

Granny was very sensible and loving, though she had special powers. She warned us you should never call up spirits because they would come if they wanted to. She said if people called up spirits, the spirit might not know how to get back and be angry or confused.

Once, my Aunty Lucy wanted to go and see a medium. My granny was upset and said she must not go, but Aunt Lucy went anyway. My granny was very angry. When Aunty Lucy got to the medium, he went into a trance but said he could not see anything except a little woman with a knife jabbing at him and telling him to keep away from her family. The medium panicked. Aunty Lucy knew it was her mother from the description.

Granny always used knives for psychic protection. If she felt someone bad was coming to the house, she crossed knives and pointed them outwards towards the door. Because we had so many visitors, earthly as well as spirits, my grandmother would cleanse the doors regularly with salt and water. She called it her spring cleaning no matter what time of the year it was.

From early childhood I could sense people's energies and would try to keep away from certain people who felt bad. At some houses I was scared because I could feel that the spirits there were not nice. Because I believed in them, good spirits would connect with me. I saw them as people or sometimes as smoke only for second, or as a shadow, as though they were moving very fast. In other houses I could smell perfume or flowers and see shadows and I would know the smell did not belong to the house but to the spirits there. I could tell my granny and she did not say I was mad but that I could see what other people could not see.

Granny said that only if a person was bad in life would they have a bad spirit and that usually it was the living who would harm us.

I only ever had two bad experiences. When I was still quite young, we moved to a house in Glasgow. As soon as we moved into the house, we knew it was wrong. Because we had had to leave Chile, we had to take the first council house we were offered. The kitchen was burned, and the old man who lived there had died. The council would not fix it, and we soon found out there were unhappy spirits there. We could hear people walking about upstairs in the front bedroom. Because we were far from home, we would try to say to each other that it was neighbours, but we knew it was not.

One night, when I was about 13, I was with the family downstairs watching television and felt I had to go upstairs. The stairs were narrow and there was no light. You had to put the light on upstairs. I was going to my room but went instead to Aunty Lucy's room. The door was open, though it was always kept shut. Inside the door I saw a hand mirror and hairbrush and went in to brush my hair. I felt someone behind me and thought it was my sister Paola playing tricks and so I said, 'Stop annoying me and come in, Paola.'

I turned round and there was a child with dark hair, who I did not know, watching me. I looked in the mirror and his reflection was there, but when I turned round again, he was not there. I could only see him in the mirror now. I went completely cold. He had no eyes. I had seen dead people and that was okay, but this was frightening. It was like slow motion. My hands went ice-cold. He was staring me from the mirror, the shape of a child, a seven-year-old boy, but he was not nice. I was in shock. I felt as if someone had hit me with a football on the head.

He was close to me and passed through me, and my heart started beating very fast. It happened in seconds, but it seemed so long. I went downstairs. Straightaway Granny knew, though I could not talk or cry nor explain. But I had seen him and felt him. Granny went upstairs and opened the windows and told the spirit to go away. Paola was younger. Soon after, she saw the same boy in her dreams and described him to me before I could describe him to her.

Another time in that house, Paola, my cousin and myself went upstairs to the toilet. We were scared to go upstairs alone, so we went with each other and waited. There were the three of us young girls in the bathroom. Suddenly, one of the handles on a door inside the bathroom started going round in circles. They were round handles, but behind the door there were no handles because the water tank was in there. It was flat behind there, and there was no space for anyone to hide. The handle continued to go round and round, and we started screaming because we could not get the bathroom door open to run away. We were screaming that we could not get out. I ran downstairs with my pants around my knees. Granny knew there was something strange happening because the light downstairs had been flickering. She got her knife and holy water to bless upstairs.

Granny used to go to church and get holy water that she kept in a jar. She put it in the room. She used a glass of water with an open pair of scissors on top over the water. On top of the scissors was red ribbon tied with bits of garlic. She left it in the bedroom for protection.

Adela's family is still very close and senses their grandmother around as a protector at times of family crisis. They hear her distinctive footsteps. She has also comforted Adela during a difficult labour.

### The fortune teller's daughter

Colleen works as a clairvoyant and astrologer on the Isle of Wight, England. Though Colleen has a full everyday life as wife, mother and businesswoman and wears suits rather than flamboyant frills for her consultations, she is rightly proud of her inheritance as a fortune teller's daughter. Her mother was a traditional clairvoyant and over the years helped holidaymakers and residents alike to make sense of their future.

My mum painted stones and cards with magical images, and we had a van and beautiful painted signs with astrology wheels. When I was eight, my mother had a booth on Ventnor Pier, and we used to play around while she worked. Then she had kiosks in Sandown and Shanklin. When I was 15, she gave me my own set of cards and taught me meditation. She told me I was the one in the family with the gift and that one day, when I was ready, I would carry on her work.

I had psychic experiences throughout my childhood. My own psychic powers grew naturally. I was never forced. Clairvoyance was just Mum's job, and before she did it professionally I think she was unhappy about not using her psychic talents.

When I was really young, I saw the eyelash people when I was in bed. My mum was in the kitchen, and the door was open. I was awake and could hear her talking to friends. On the wall beside me I could see a stick table and on it a family of eyelash people who were made of eyelashes. They were four or five inches tall and flew down and pulled out my eyelashes. They would pull one and take it back to the table, then later take another one. They must have taken six in all. I was frightened but very excited. Eventually, I called my mother. Though she could not see them, she gave me a china tiger to protect me. I still have it. After that, although I was aware of them at the table in my bedroom, they could not come and get me.

There was one house in Whitwell, where we lived for a time, that was haunted. The house stood on its own. We moved into it when I was about four. My mother was convinced it was built on water, and it turned out that it was on the site of an old reservoir [known to cause psychic disturbances because of the negative psychic energy streams running through such land]. Lots of strange things happened there. My brothers and I shared a huge bedroom, and one night we saw two or three fairies fly out of the fireplace and in up the chimney again. They were a few inches high and flew. They were like lights with circles of light around them that got paler as it went outwards.

Doors would open and shut by themselves, and electrical lights would switch on and off, but we were never aware of any negative energies. But things would go wrong in the house, and we did not settle. My dad had a security firm and police dogs, and they would go mad in the house and garden, so eventually we sold it. I recall that the garden was huge, and I used to see a well, not the wishing well kind but a hole with water there.

From when I was young I could always make things happen or, if I wanted to see someone, get them to call or phone with my mind. As I got older, Mother taught me to look in the mirror and let my face change. When I grew up, my mediumistic gifts developed, so I could get messages for people who had lost relatives and let them see their loved ones in my face.

But even as a child I could always pick up what people were feeling, especially if they were sad or unwell. At school everyone thought what my mother did was fabulous, but I just wanted to be ordinary. If people did not know me or who my mother was, I would dress normally, and I was a hairdresser until I was 24.

Colleen now uses her mother's beautiful cards and stones in her psychic work and has her own exquisitely painted astrological board and signs.

## The boy who loved flowers

There are those who believe that healing is a natural gift that cannot be taught. Young children are often natural healers, but healing abilities may be lost or become dormant along with other psychic powers when children start school. Rarely, however, does a young person devote their life to healing at an age when other children are out playing games after school. Takaaki, the young Japanese healer, was a perfectly ordinary child before he was given what he considers his mission.

Takaaki is the only person in this chapter I have not met personally. I am therefore indebted to my dear Japanese friend Atushi, a man of great learning and wisdom, for helping me to discover Takaaki's story and for spending hours translating papers and transcribing information for me. Atushi also sent grapes, the speciality of his own region, to Takaaki by way of thanks for his cooperation.

This is an unusual story in that Takaaki's parents supported him financially and emotionally and protected him so that he was able to develop his gifts in his own way and at his own pace and was not exploited commercially. He also showed great maturity in wanting to help others and still going to school like an ordinary teenager.

I first learned of Takaaki Moor in 1995, when he was a 17-year-old senior high school student in Japan. Each afternoon he rushed home from school to heal the sick and distressed waiting outside his door. Between 30 and 40 patients would be waiting every day, but the teenager would accept no money at all for his activities. Takaaki would accept only flowers, which he loves, and sometimes fruit.

When Takaaki was 11, he received what he described as a revelation of the Buddha in the spring of 1990. A white light flashed out of the family altar, and from the light a quiet voice told Takaaki that he would be given superhuman powers and that he had been chosen by the Buddha to heal illnesses. Takaaki believes that it was the Buddha himself who spoke. Takaaki went into the kitchen, where his mother was preparing supper and told her of his vision. His mother would not believe him, but at last agreed that if he could cure her painful and persistent headaches, then she would accept his words.

Takaaki found that he could see inside his mother's head and that part of her brain was crimson. He prayed that the bad part would be cured. The Buddha's voice told him to call out three times for the pain to depart. This Takaaki did. Gradually the crimson colour disappeared and his mother never again suffered from headaches.

From that moment Takaaki's healing work began. He healed friends and acquaintances of the family, both in their presence and in their absence. Mr Yoshi, an acquaintance of his father's, had come to the office dragging his leg and in great pain. Takaaki's father asked for Mr Yoshi's business card, promising that his son would cure the leg by absent healing.

That evening, as Takaaki held the card, a severe pain coursed through his own left leg. When Takaaki put down the card, the pain disappeared. Then, as though on a television screen, Takaaki was able to see an image and realised that the spirit of someone who had died was hanging on to Mr Yoshi's leg. The spirit revealed that he was a good friend who had died but did not want to leave someone of whom he had been especially fond in life. Takaaki explained to the spirit that he was unintentionally hurting his former friend and so the spirit agreed to depart.

The pain ceased immediately. Later, Mr Yoshi told Takaaki's father that he had recently lost a very close friend and had been chief mourner at his funeral. It was soon after this death that the pain had started.

To some Western minds, such a concept might sound strange, but there are many ways of expressing the complex link between not only our own bodies and minds but also those to whom we are bonded in love.

Takaaki says that at first the Buddha helped him when he did not know what to do, because he was still a child, but gradually his own powers have taken over the healing processes.

Takaaki is now 25 years old, I was anxious to find out whether his gifts had continued and whether he had been affected by his growing fame. Atushi spoke to Takaaki's mother on my behalf. She reported that her son's healing powers have greatly increased, and he now travels to Tokyo and Osaka by plane for weekly consultations. However, he still does much good in his own region and has, as far as I can ascertain, kept his original innocence and integrity in spite of his celebrity.

## The gypsy witch

*Sabrina the Teenage Witch* and *Buffy the Vampire Slayer*, along with a plethora of teen spell books, have caused an upsurge in interest in teenage magic. However, many young people are drawn to the more serious side of Wicca, for – in spite of lurid images in the popular imagination of witches dancing naked on moorland and brewing up hideous potions of bats and rats – this is a responsible religion in which the basic tenet is respect for all life forms and for the natural rhythms of the seasons and of the earth.

Melody is now in her twenties, the owner of a New Age store in Winchester, England, and a practicing Wiccan. She does a lot of work helping young people to understand the spiritual and ethical aspects of witchcraft and countering the more sensational and erroneous popular images derived from films such as *The Craft* and *Practical Magic*.

Melody was not brought up in Wicca but discovered it when she was a teenager. However, her childhood is unusual in that it was spent in harmony with nature and with strong influence from Romany spiritual beliefs.

My grandfather was a Romany and built my grandmother a bungalow before my father, Tom, was born. Unfortunately, he didn't finish it in time, so my father was born Romany-style in the caravan.

My grandparents had a smallholding with chickens, goats and a donkey. Every Sunday I would go and see my grandparents. They had special things from the Romany days hidden away in the back room. In the corner was a massive staff with red, white and black wool around the spearhead. Granddad said that it belonged to a medicine man who had blessed the house. I was not supposed to touch the staff, but when no one was around, I took three strands of wool and made them into a bracelet round my wrist, as I was sure that would protect me.

My granddad used to take me round his land and teach me about different kinds of herbs. He allowed me to eat different kinds of apples, so I learned which were good for eating, which for cooking and which could be used medicinally. He once gave me a really sour crab apple, and when I spat it out, he laughed and said, 'Now you know never to eat one of those.' If I stung myself, he showed me the waxy dock leaf to put on it. He would also show me which herb was rosemary to cook with, chamomile for calming tea and sage for healing. My grandfather knew when it would be a hard winter or an early spring and passed on the old weather and countryside lore to me.

My grandma was wonderful with animals and could heal anything just by touching it. People used to bring her sick or injured animals, and she would nurse them back to health.

Through the years I learned to trust my psychic instincts, because my grandfather was so tuned in. For example, the night before my granddad had a serious accident, he turned up at our house late in the evening. Though we were in bed, he insisted on getting us up and playing with us. He was skipping round the house and dancing like a child. He talked to me especially. The following morning he was working high up a tree (he was a tree surgeon, a job he had done for 40 years). He fell and became paralysed and never walked again.

The psychic powers skipped a generation and came to me. Dad, the eldest of the three children, lived quite a conventional life and became a landscape gardener. He was Church of England and my natural mother was Roman Catholic. Romany people have strict ethics and generally belong to a Christian church. When I was 13 or 14 I tried Buddhism. I was at a Church of England school and felt I should be religious. I tried different churches but I loved the philosophy of Buddhism and seeing the world in a karmic ever-turning circle.

My sister Victoria died when I was eight. Then things started to happen. Objects in the house would move and break, and my parents were always angry with me. I said it was Victoria, but they would not believe me. Electric appliances would switch on and off. The family had a meeting behind closed doors, and I eavesdropped. My grandmother, grandfather, stepmother and father were there. My grandmother said I was using telekinesis, the power of the mind to move things unconsciously. I felt betrayed by my parents talking about me behind closed doors, because I knew it was Victoria moving those things. I could see spirits and know things even then.

So it is very strange that when I was 14 my stepmother bought me a set of Tarot cards. I loved the pictures on the cards and made a bag for them with an old red silk shirt because you are supposed to keep Tarot in silk. Years before, my stepmother had made herself a set of runes and occasionally read them and laid them out on the bed. Then, when I was in my teens, something bad must have happened because she suddenly stopped reading them. I remember I kept three of the runes as lucky charms.

I would give friends readings with my cards. The Tarot readings I gave for my friends were always accurate, but the ones for myself were quite murky, though they said things would get better. Because I had younger brothers and sisters, my Tarot readings were never discussed at home. In my later teens I gave my stepmother readings. Again, it is strange that she asked in view of her mixed feelings.

From the age of 14 I was into the occult and spirits, spell-casting, scrying and pendulum dowsing. When I was 16 I started to explore Wicca. I was dabbling with ideas, not practising the religion as such. It was not till I was about 18 that I took up the Wiccan path formally, having realised I was doing all the Wiccan things without giving them a name.

My acceptance that I was a witch came after a sad incident. My friend Anna became pregnant. One morning, at about 10 am, I was hit as if by a sonic boom and the walls came out and went in again. I was doubled up in pain. I knew that Anna was losing the baby. I told another friend at 2 pm that Anna had lost the baby. She told me I should not even think such things, let alone say them.

At 2 pm, Pete, Anna's boyfriend, phoned to say she was in hospital. I found out later that at 10 am she had been doubled up in pain and at 2 pm she had been told she had lost the baby. I wanted to see Anna. When I told her about sharing her pain, she hit me over the head with a Wiccan book and said, 'Girl, you are a witch. Deal with it.'

I realised then I had been practising witchcraft for four years but had never admitted what I was to myself, let alone anyone else. Now I live by a spiritual path in which my business life is enhanced by my strong belief in the power to change life for the better and the responsibilities involved in doing so. And I don't ride a broomstick.

## The young witch growing up in the Craft

Kore is 19 and was brought up in the Wiccan tradition of witchcraft. In my own experience, children who are brought up in this tradition are invariably kind and have great respect for nature and for other people. They also tend to be non-materialistic and environmentally aware. Wiccan children are not involved formally in any spiritual practices until adulthood, and even then are expected to make up their own mind about their spiritual path.

I was born in 1983 and welcomed by the Wiccan faith two weeks later, on the spring equinox sabbat (seasonal celebration), on 20 March. I was never told that it was the one true way or that I had to be a part of it. I was encouraged to learn about other religions to give me the broader view. Nor was I ever pressurised to take part in any ritual or other Wiccan activity. In fact, my mother had more of a job trying to keep me out of it.

My earliest memories of Wicca are mainly of bonfires at Beltane (May eve) and parties at Halloween.

I never attended full moon meetings, nor was I involved in any practical witchcraft until I was much older. I did attend sabbats, which I thought were great fun, and I enjoyed the extra festivities we had. I loved all the preparations for the festivals, going out to collect the greenery to make offerings to the trees. The earth was a living and magical place, full of gods, goddesses and nature spirits.

When I started primary school, it didn't occur to me that the other children were not brought up the same. I remember on a few occasions talking to my friends about being a witch even though the teachers had said I shouldn't.

I was regularly reminded by my mother of the need for discretion and that not everybody was open-minded about such matters. My parents had told the teachers at school about my religion, and they were not overly concerned. It was a Church of England school, and I was given the choice whether I wanted to take part in certain religious activities or not. My mother had said that all the gods and goddesses are the same, just with different names, and anyway I didn't want to be the only one left out. On one occasion I was asked to leave the class, which was being taught by the local vicar, for saying rather loudly that smearing lambs' blood around doors on the first Passover wasn't very nice,

The only problems came when I went to secondary school. I became a teenager with the usual attitude. I disagreed frequently with my religious education teacher, and he didn't like the fact I was a Wiccan at all. In secondary school for the first three years I was teased and called names.

But by the time I was 15, the first teen witch books had arrived on the market. Television programmes like 'Sabrina the Teenage Witch' appeared on our television screens, and almost overnight witchcraft was the fashion. I was very happy about this at the time, as I thought I would be able to chat about it to my friends. But I was disappointed. All my friends were taking up palm-reading and Tarot, but Wicca is a very spiritual religion and not just about spells, so it had no real interest for them at all.

After I left school, I went to college and now am at university. I only discuss my religion with people who are genuinely interested. I am still asked if I can fly a broomstick. The single most important thing I feel being brought up in Wicca has given me is that I have never had to deal with the fear of death because I know life goes on.

## The boy who lived with nature

This is perhaps the strangest childhood account I have ever come across. Had I not known Andrew personally as a logical, macho, sometimes cynical business person with an atrocious sense of humour and a liking for fast motorbikes, I might have dismissed his story as a fantasy.

I wrote about Andrew's enduring link with his winged lion Haimayne on page 69. But Haimayne was no ordinary, fun, invisible friend. He taught the solitary boy all about nature and magic and acted as a mentor to him in the Somerset countryside around Shepton Mallet.

Andrew had a relatively unusual childhood. His parents left him largely to bring himself up and to wander where he wished. Sometimes they went away for a week or more when he was quite young, leaving him alone with what seems to me, as a city-bred person, very little adult supervision. Without this high level of unsupervised freedom, Haimayne would not have been able to occupy so much of his life.

Had Andrew lived in a town instead of deep country, neither would he have had access to the wild places that he made his childhood playground. Andrew has immense knowledge of nature and also of magic, but he has no real idea how, had it not been for Haimayne, he would have learned these things in childhood, for there was no library nearby, and he found school learning very difficult and rather pointless.

I was solitary and knew no other children before junior school. Even then no one lived near me, and so I was largely alone, because I was an only child and my parents left me to my own devices.

When I was very young, I was drawn to this strange place that was a long walk from my home for a young child. People called it the Place of the Dead. You stepped down into the woods, and there were no birds and no wildlife. There was an old ruined mansion and an abandoned village. Many years before, there had been a terrible tragedy. Part of the quarry owner's house had collapsed, and the family were killed. The owner had never forgiven himself, and after a few years could bear it no more and committed suicide. The quarry was shut down and the people went away. I set up a play park there because to me it was not frightening but wild and beautiful and totally magical. There were old gazebos and lakes. There was a 150-foot [45-metre] rock with two oak trees on top that looked like a bearded man's face with antlers. I would play between the two trees on the top.

Haimayne smelled strong like a lion and was brown and yellowy, velvety, but was skin and bone. Though he had wings, he never flew. I was grown up when my sister Becky was born and only saw her rarely. I went to see the family once when she was three-and-a-half, and Becky told me about her winged lion. But I never asked her what they did together, because she was not part of my life, as I was so much older and did not go home. I have never asked. I know Becky lost her Haimayne when she was somewhere between 12 and 15. It was the same time she started playing the guitar.

Haimayne didn't hold conversations as such with me or talk about trivia. He would laugh, the kind of loud raucous laugh that in humans has others turning round to stare. He would tell me what to do and how to pronounce words we needed for our rituals. I wrote these down in what I called my glossary.

When I first met Haimayne, he told me we had work to do, and I did not like work. Work was school. But this was very different. And it was so much harder. But it had a point.

I never thought of Haimayne as invisible. There was an old Catholic scholar who lived in a cottage I passed on walks, and when I was alone, he would ask, 'And where are you two off to today?' I think he must have seen Haimayne, though I never spoke of him to anyone.

Haimayne would only come into the house if he was invited. Sometimes he would knock on the door. We had a huge brass knocker, and I would know it was him. My Dad would answer and look up and down, because he could not see anyone outside. Haimayne would be there giving one of his funny looks, and my mother, who would not even look up, would say, 'Come in then, if you're coming.'

Haimayne would scuttle in and up to my bedroom, and we would make plans. We were always going amazing places, even when I was young. We would open my window and climb out and be gone for hours or days in the holidays. My parents never asked or worried if I was there or not and sometimes went away themselves.

Before an adventure, Haimayne would tell me what we needed – salt, matches, something to write on (there was always slate around the area), chalk to write with on the slate, sometimes berries.

When we were going travelling, we had to prepare a tablet either of clay or wax the night before as a protective charm. It took ages to prepare. I used my grandfather's old tobacco tin filled with clay and straw or wax. The following morning one side would still be soft, and we could press into it the journey plan. A figure to represent me, a small person for Haimayne, a vertical line to indicate the path of the travel and equals signs for the time we would stay away. We would leave the tablet over the stile in the hawthorn tree, where water came from the ground in the crown of the first hawthorn cleft. It was like leaving a note saying when we could be found, and as long as it was undisturbed, we could come back safely. Afterwards we would get rid of the map by burning it.

The time I fell from the cliff and Haimayne saved me (see page 69), was the only time the branch had cracked in half and the tablet had fallen. The branch was strong enough to sit in. When we got home and discovered it, we picked up the pieces that had fallen on the ground and burned them.

From the time I was about six, when he came into my life, Haimayne was my teacher and best mate, but he also lied and played tricks to teach me things. He would say, 'Put your finger in that hole.' I remember once a sharp-toothed vole bit me. Haimayne laughed and said that is why you should never put your fingers in a hole.

He told me you should always walk upstream to find fresh water because they buried people in rivers, and he explained about sewing people into bags. I couldn't understand, because people were buried in churchyards, but he said that was now.

Haimayne taught me spells and chants, water divination and woodcraft about the trees and what you could use the woods for. He would show me how to pull up foxgloves and not get stains on my hands, as they were poisonous. Haimayne told me about poisons and what was safe to eat, and how a certain call meant that a bird was nesting nearby. This meant that if we were hungry we could get an egg and cook it.

When I was 11, he taught me how to use candles and mirrors to look through time. Each had to be precisely aligned and, as an adult, others have commented on the complex mathematical processes involved in my early diagrams that I have kept. Looking back at these, we always used pictograms or strange marks when we were writing our spells, though Haimayne did help me to read and write. There were special words in my glossary book for the four directions and the stars, for ghosts and for saving lost souls. They weren't another language really, just written how I was told to pronounce them by Haimayne. Though I found formal learning difficult, Haimayne made me pronounce things over and over to get them right.

I found as an adult that I knew all about trees, birds, herbs, flowers and old places. It was just that the names I was taught were different from the ones I have seen as an adult, but the information was all true and far beyond the grasp of a young boy, except I did learn it then.

On my thirteenth birthday I was due at a school event, but it was cancelled, and I took the day off. Haimayne and I said goodbye, and we had a conversation about him going. I said it would give me more time for other things. As an adult I talk about Haimayne as if he is a deceased friend of whom I am very fond.

Andrew has grown up to succeed in the world's terms but has kept his free spirit and has sometimes turned his back on materialism for periods, for example to walk around the coastline of Britain. Had Andrew been caught in the net of social intervention or educational psychologists as a child, the story and the outcome might have been very different.

How can we explain this strange story? Was Andrew somehow tapping into a source of collective wisdom? Who was Haimayne and why did he stay so long? Is it significant that he so closely resembled a Babylonian sphinx (see page 70), a creature depicted by a people famed for their magical and astrological lore thousands of years ago? Why did he return to Andrew's sister? I have seen some of Andrew's amazingly advanced childhood scribblings and intend to investigate further.

### The third-generation clairvoyant

This is the story of my good friend Lilian, healer, clairvoyant, past-life regressionist, white witch, mother and grandmother.

About 17 years ago, in what Lilian calls my sensible days, I was absolutely petrified to be interviewing a white witch and really expected her to come flying in on her broomstick. But throughout our relationship she has usually been the sensible one, with her common sense and down-to-earth advice when my world was spinning out of control.

Lilian is a third-generation clairvoyant. She had two psychic grandmothers, and her mother and father both had the gift of second sight. She had an idyllic, magical, working-class childhood, in which she was loved and grew up knowing that cauldrons were good for making Irish stew and fairies also had to go home at bedtime.

Lilian now lives in a chalet in a beautiful garden on the borders of Berkshire and Surrey, England. People come to her for help and advice, a Tarot or crystal ball reading, just as they came to her mother and grandmothers when more conventional methods of coping with the world failed.

Unlike some of the people I have written about, who were disbelieved as children or punished when they spoke of seeing ghosts or foretold the future, Lilian was brought up in an atmosphere that cheerfully accepted the supernatural as just another facet of life – which it is. At one stage of her childhood, Lilian was a very devout Christian, and this faith co-existed quite happily with the other assorted beliefs she had acquired.

Lilian was born in 1937, and, when she was two, the family moved from Manchester to a little village in Cheshire. Lilian told me:

> The cottage had a thatched roof and dirt floor. I can remember Dad laying a proper floor. It was called Holly Cottage. There was a pump outside and a stone two feet [60 centimetres] high on the floor by the fireplace.

The cottage was built around this stone. When Lilian visited the cottage years later, she saw that, although her former home had been modernised and the thatch was gone, the stone in the centre was still there. Lilian always thought of it as a magic stone in her childhood.

One of her first memories was of an invisible friend, an ancient Egyptian girl, although she can't remember her name. Lilian says she was about three years old when the Egyptian girl came into her life:

> The Egyptian girl was very close to me, like a sister. She said you had to wear your plaits in front of the shoulders to denote rank. I can still recall the place she used to take me, the tall rushes and water and beautiful flowers growing on top of the water, like water lilies but prettier.

Her mother recalled how Lilian used to come out with all sorts of information about ancient Egypt that she could not possibly have known at that age. But as Lilian grew older, her invisible friend faded. Lilian is still attracted by Egypt.

During the wartime Blitz, Lilian's grannies moved in with her family. They both read the teacups, and Lilian's house became the place for local people to come to seek knowledge of the future:

> Granny Burton, Dad's mother, was Irish and read the playing cards as well as the teacups. She was a powerful woman but very pretty, with her white hair streaked with golden strands. Granny Leonard was tiny, very prim and proper, with aspirations to being middle class.
>
> When I was little, I used to show off at tea leaf reading sessions and by three or four years old had developed my own clientele. 'Let the little one do the reading,' people used to say.

Both the grandmas were strong believers in rules for the reading of the teacups, and Lilian was made to learn and obey them.

Rule 1: Do not acknowledge people to whom you've given readings when you meet them on the street unless they speak first.

Rule 2: Try not to see anything unavoidably bad and do not worry the clients. (Lilian says the conditioning of Granny Leonard and Granny Burton was so strong she didn't see anything bad – and still doesn't.)

Rule 3: If you do see anything avoidably bad, try to see how it can be averted for your client.

Granny Burton was Lilian's special teacher. She used to watch her reading the cups and ask, 'Where did you see that, child?' When Lilian showed her, Granny Burton would poke at the leaves with her fingers and then say, 'Carry on, child.' Lilian says:

> I went to a local school for a while but didn't like it as it was so dull. So I changed to another school right opposite the church. The local vicar was very nice to me and took a marked interest in me, perhaps because of the family reputation with the tea leaves.

Following the family tradition, from the age of five Lilian began casting love spells of her own in the playground:

> One of the children would say, 'Do a spell,' and immediately I would create one. At that time love was in short supply. The war was on, and parents were very busy, often with dads away fighting. I always had a gift for poetry, so I found it very easy to make up a song or a chorus and get the other children in the playground to dance in and out in a chain dance. Then I would throw the wish into the middle. Sometimes the petitioner stood in the middle as well.

The spells gave Lilian confidence at school and made her very popular.

When Lilian was nearly seven, a shadow was discovered on her lungs, and she had well over a year off school. She also caught whooping cough and scarlet fever and was taken to see a specialist in Chester, whose only suggestion for treatment was that she should be allowed to live outdoors as much as possible.

> I ran wild. I was left to my own devices and started to see things in a different way. I got very close to nature and began to be aware of natural presences. The grandmothers had settled back in Manchester after the Blitz, so they only came on visits, but I used to discuss the presences with my mother.

Lilian should have been learning to read and write and do arithmetic, but she thinks this lack of formal education gave her time for the other psychic areas of her brain to come out – and being clever she soon caught up. When she was 14, Lilian won a scholarship to an art school.

> I realised that I had to be careful not put myself in the line of ridicule, so I played down my psychic abilities. It was a real culture shock to go to art college. For a time I forgot about doing spells, as other people couldn't do them.

Somewhere around this time, Lilian was introduced to the Tarot cards and took to them straight away. She had always read playing cards, taught by Granny Burton, so this was just one step on from that. She remembers, 'Tarot readings were considered more permissible in college society.'

At the age of 17, Lilian came south, determined not to let anyone know she was psychic:

> I would just be an ordinary person and not let on about my powers, but I found that complete strangers at odd times somehow guessed that I knew things and could make predictions.

Lilian married young and by 19 had had her first child. She gave the odd reading during this time and gradually built up a clientele.

Many mothers experience a psychic link with their first child that they had never suspected could exist, but Lilian, for all her intuitive skills, found herself as nervous as any other first-time mother:

> My eldest child completely blew my brains. I was so desperate to be a perfect mum that I ignored my psyche. I used to get up every hour during the night and hold a glass in front of my daughter's face to see if she was still breathing. By the second child, I'd got my act together. If Peg was restless, I could send thoughts to calm her down. With all the younger ones I could send thoughts to the cot or pram from wherever I was to stop them crying.

### The clairvoyant's daughter

Lesley, Lilian's youngest daughter, is the one who has followed most closely in her mother's psychic footsteps. Lesley is an actress by profession but also organises psychic fairs. From childhood, Lesley read the runes and the Tarot as part of her ordinary life.

Lilian's children were, like her, brought up in the countryside. Lesley told me:

> It was really beautiful where we lived, and we children used the countryside as our garden. It seemed very magical. We lived in an old house at a crossroads. There was a deserted lane and a big mansion that used to be a sanatorium. We played in the garden. We used to call it the Japanese or magic garden. There was a magical lake, and we ran inside the empty house. We had lots of bird friends and used to talk to them.
>
> When it was sunset, we used to hear the drummer in the sky beating the drums, and we knew it was time to go home. The sunset would come up, and we had to get home before the sunset went over our heads. We would run down the little hill fast as we could and always made it.
>
> We used to see misty figures, and my sister Peg often saw ghosts. There was a house down the road that was haunted. Peg stayed in her friend's bedroom and once woke to see a blue lady drinking a cup of tea sitting on the bed. Another time, in the same bedroom, Peg looked up and saw a man in a turban with a sword, waving it above her head. Peg was about eight at the time, and I was a year younger.
>
> Another time, Peg came dashing into our house to tell me to come and see the ghosts. There were two pillars we used to climb on, marking the entrance where a big gate once was. There were four ghosts sitting on the pillars. They were four children.

Lesley's interest in runes began in her childhood.

> When I was young, I used to throw stones and twigs and made amulets and charms with them. Everything was a ritual. I used to see the past and future with the runes I made. I created my own meanings for the symbols I put on them. I could tell who a person's family was before I knew them and could always see their parents. I would sometimes read my runes for friends and family, but I mainly preferred to play with them by myself. I knew stones to be magic and powerful. You have to let the ability develop naturally.

Lesley says she could tell the future but in the family tradition would not foretell doom, only give warnings.

> I did not realise I was brought up differently from other kids until I was about 25. Mum was very in tune with the universal laws. She

did spells at home. But when Mum stepped into school on open nights, some of the girls were quite scared of her. Her blonde hair was fluffed out, and she would wear flowing dresses with huge mediaeval sleeves. She used to waltz into school. People would say, 'Wow! Is that your mother?' One woman used to cross herself when she passed our house.

Lesley started giving Tarot readings at the age of about eight, and her friends would come to her for readings. She also helped people through astrology.

People were always coming to Mum for sessions of clairvoyance and to ask her advice. People would come knocking on the door at all hours for tea leaf readings or healing.

Mum would do spells on the new moon, but they were always positive ones, to make good things happen for people. I remember we would sing songs and go on adventures together with Mum, jumping over streams, picking flowers and eating fresh herbs. Sometimes at night I would see her in the garden dancing round the flowers. Mine was a good childhood.

There was nothing secret or spooky about Lesley and Lilian's world. Some may disapprove of a childhood removed from the mainstream, in a world where nature is central and material goods are secondary. However, such a lifestyle may be no bad antidote to a world in which childhood hyperactivity is increasing and many children are addicted to violent computer games.

# CHAPTER 11

# Where the Magic Goes

This is a book close to my heart, not just because the original edition was the first book I ever wrote but also because it is on a subject that, over the years, has given me a chance to share special moments in people's lives.

Over time I have become even more open-minded about psychic matters and have realised that life is infinitely more amazing and wonderful than ever I imagined when I struggled to make sense of my son Jack's experiences within a hopelessly inadequate psychological framework. I am no longer so daunted by sceptics and scientists demanding proof on the television or radio programmes on which I appear. Like a strong-beaked mother hen, I defend my accounts and the people who have shared them with me, because they have so much significance for the people who told them to me. If we accept only what can be verified by independent witnesses or tested under laboratory conditions, then we have a very narrow view of the universe. I still recall a physicist, actually a very nice man off-screen, demanding why I hadn't taken a photograph of my mother's ghost when she came back to visit me after she had died traumatically of cancer when I was only 19.

Jack, who started my career, is now 20 and making a good career of his own in the hospitality industry. He has a gift with people and, though he no longer predicts the future, he is still sensitive to my moods. He will phone spontaneously if I am sad or unwell, even if he is many miles away, to bring sunshine into my world. However, contacting him about more mundane matters is harder than getting through to the Queen.

I have five children, nearly grown up but always in my heart – and my cheque book. I have shared their magical moments, their invisible friends, their mind-hopping powers, their angels, their phantom foes and their out-of-the-blue spot-on predictions, forgotten moments later. I wish I had recorded them all, but there is never time. I have also seen the magic of my own childhood re-emerge as I write, no longer stored away and tidied up by my sensible mind. I know now that some of the experiences dismissed by my parents as imagination really did happen to me. For that reason I have especially treasured experiences from older people who can look back and say that, yes, it really was true all those years ago. Occasionally, retelling a story in which they were punished for their psychic terrors has helped them at least to acknowledge the injustices done to them, sometimes because the parent did not know what to do or was damaged themselves by their own childhood.

I hope that this book is of some help to parents of children who have psychic experiences and will reassure them that their children are quite normal. I hope also that child professionals who read it will feel more confident to deal with the children they encounter who talk about ghosts or invisible friends – and more able to use these precious confidences as a way of exploring with the child their everyday fears and needs.

It is important that children's psychic experiences aren't just the subject of spooky articles and programmes, though these can be a good way of allowing other people to know that their own – perhaps secret – experiences are shared by others. Teenagers especially should have access to a sensible antidote to the teen-spell hype so that they do not experiment furtively with ouija boards and then feel afraid to tell adults if they scare themselves. A few people will still say that books like this are evil and we shouldn't be dabbling. Some psychologists say I am wrong to encourage people to believe that psychic experiences are not all in their mind.

But how can it be wrong or incredible that a deceased grandmother wants to come back occasionally and watch over her grandchildren? Love never dies. How can guardian angels and spirit guides be other than benign? Isn't it wonderful that our children care for us so much that they can pop into our thoughts, even if this may be a little inconvenient at times? If our children get frightened – and we can unconsciously pass on our own fears of death and ghosts – then this is a good opportunity to help them with their earthly fears as well.

Psychological or psychic the encounter may be – perhaps a bit of both in many cases. Children do come, as William Wordsworth put it, 'trailing clouds of glory'. We can learn much just by listening and seeing life though a child's eyes for a moment or two.

If you have young children, do record their precious insights. When your child leaves home or becomes a parent, you can pass on the recollections so that they know how loved they are and how precious were those childhood moments.

It is nearly the witching hour, and I am sitting writing these final words as the rain pours down over the darkened caravan site where I escape to my battered but much loved caravan to write. I still occasionally get spooked by the darkness and by fears in my head that take on phantasmal forms in shadowy corners. Then it will be my turn to phone my children – who now tower over me physically and outpace me at every turn – for reassurance that the clanking I can hear is the temperamental boiler and not the rattling of ghostly chains. What is more, no self-respecting spectre or headless huntsman would be lurking soaking wet in the hedgerow outside, waiting for me to put out the rubbish.

If any of you would like to write to me with experiences or questions I may be able to help with, you can do so via my website, at www.cassandraeason.co.uk. I rarely get time to write letters, but am better at answering e-mails.

# Further Reading

### Angels and spirit guides

Newcomb, Jacky, *An Angel Treasury: A collection of encounters, inspirations and heavenly love,* Element Books (Thorsons), 2004
Roland, Paul, *Contact Your Guardian Angel,* Foulsham/Quantum, 2004
White, Ruth, *Working with Spirit Guides,* Piatkus, 2004

### Childhood spirituality

Lee, Carroll, and Tober, Jan, *Indigo Children,* Hay House, 2001
Doe, Mimi, and Walch, Marsha, *Nourishing Your Child's Soul: Ten principles of spiritual parenting,* Harper Collins, US, 1998
Virtue, Doreen, *Crystal Children: A guide to the newest generation of psychic and sensitive children,* Hay House, 2003

### Crystals

Eason, Cassandra, *Illustrated Dictionary of Healing Crystals,* Sterling, New York, 2003, Collins and Brown, 2004
Bourgault, Luc, *The American Indian Secrets of Crystal Healing,* Foulsham/Quantum, 1997

### Dreams

Eason, Cassandra, *Modern Book of Dream Interpretation,* Foulsham/Quantum 2005
Jaskolka, Anna, *Teen Dreams and What They Mean,* Foulsham/Quantum, 2003
Melbourne, David, and Hearne, Dr Keith, *The Dream Oracle,* Foulsham/Quantum, 2002

### Energy work, auras and chakras

Brennan, Barbara Ann, *Hands of Light: A guide to healing through the human energy field,* Bantam Books, US, 1987
Eason, Cassandra, *Aura Reading,* Piatkus, 2000
Eason, Cassandra, *Chakra Power,* Foulsham/Quantum, 2002

## Extra-terrestrial encounters

Boylan, Richard, (1999, Winter) Academy of Clinical Close Encounter Therapists (ACCET) Newsletter, 'Star Kids Benefit From Special Schooling.' At: http://www3.eu.spiritweb.org/spirit/richard-boylan.html

Randles, Jenny, *The Complete Book of Aliens and Abductions,* Piatkus, 2000

Wilson, Colin, *Alien Dawn: An investigation into the contact experience,* Virgin Publishing, 1998

## Fairies

Bruce, Marie, *Faerie Magick,* Foulsham/Quantum, 2005

Cooper, Joe, *The Cottingley Fairies,* Simon and Schuster, 1998

Cross, TP, and Slover, CH, *Ancient Irish Tales,* Barnes and Noble Books, 1996

Eason, Cassandra, *Complete Guide to Fairies and Magical Beings,* Piatkus 2000, Red/Wheel Weiser, US, 2002

## Past lives

Eason, Cassandra, *Discover Your Past Lives,* Foulsham/Quantum, 1995

Stevenson, Ian, *Children Who Remember Previous Lives: A question of reincarnation,* McFarland and Co., US, 2000

## Psychic children

Choquette, Sonia, *The Wise Child: A spiritual guide to nurture your child's intuition,* Three Rivers Press, US, 1999

Dong, Paul, and Raffill, Thomas, *China's Super Psychics,* Marlowe and Co., US, 1997

Jones, Carl, *From Parent to Child: The psychic link,* Warner Books, 1989

## Near-death experiences

Morse, Melvin and Paul Perry, *Closer to the Light: Learning from children's near death experiences,* Souvenir Press, 1991

## The mother–child bond

Eason, Cassandra, *The Mother Link,* Ulysses Press, US, 1999

## Mary Rodwell of ACERN

Mary Rodwell is Principal of the Australian Close Encounter Resource Network (ACERN). She can be contacted by phone/fax on (0061) 08 9385 7795 or by e-mail at starline@iinet.net.au.

# Index